Rainbow English Programme for P...

Above the Clouds!

Portfolio Book

MERIEL McCORD DEIRDRE MULLIGAN
KEVIN BARRY ANDRÉE MULVIHILL

STAGE 4
BOOK 1

CJ Fallon
ESTABLISHED 1895

Published by
CJ Fallon
Ground Floor – Block B
Liffey Valley Office Campus
Dublin 22

ISBN: 978-0-7144-2718-8

First Edition May 2019
This Reprint February 2024

© CJ Fallon

All rights reserved.

No part of this publication may be reproduced or transmitted, in any form or by any means, electronic, mechanical, photocopying or otherwise, without the prior written permission of the publisher.

Printed in Ireland by
W&G Baird Limited
Caulside Drive
Antrim BT41 2RS

The paper stock used in this publication comes from managed forests. This means that at least one tree is planted for every tree felled. The inks used for printing are environmentally friendly and vegetable based.

Introduction

This ground-breaking **Portfolio Book** accompanies the core book *Above the Clouds!* It reinforces the comprehension, vocabulary, word study/phonics, grammar and punctuation covered in the core book. A unique feature of the Portfolio Book is that it covers all the **writing genres**. All writing activities/genres are modelled in the dedicated **online writing activities** section. The Portfolio Book is a clear record of the student's work for the year.

The Writing Genres

1. **Recount writing:** tells about the events in the order in which they happened. You can recount stories or events from storybooks, diaries, newspaper articles, history books and eyewitness accounts.

2. **Report writing:** describes and gives clear information about objects, places, animals or people. You can make reports on newspaper articles, fiction or non-fiction books, games, meetings, races, a robbery, accidents, school sports day, parades and concerts.

3. **Explanatory writing:** explains how or why things occur. Examples of explanatory writing can be found in science books, on the internet, non-fiction books, SESE books or in encyclopedias.

4. **Narrative writing:** entertains and engages the reader in an imaginative experience. It includes the character(s), the setting and the event(s) leading to a problem and a solution to the same problem. Examples of narrative writing can be found in storybooks, novels, fairy tales, fables, myths, legends, plays and poems.

5. **Persuasive writing:** is used to persuade others by involving argument and debate. Persuasive writing should have an introduction to the topic, a middle section discussing the topic in more depth and must finish with a final conclusion. Examples of persuasive writing are in debates, book and film reviews and advertisements.

6. **Writing to socialise:** is used to maintain or enhance relationships. It can be formal or informal, depending on the relationship between the writer and the audience, e.g. postcards, letters, emails, texts, notes of apology, invitations and messages.

7. **Procedural writing:** contains a set of step-by-step instructions for doing something, e.g. a recipe or list of instructions for operating a machine, etc. Examples of procedural writing can be found in recipe and cookery books, assembly kits, rules for games, science books and maps.

8. **Free writing:** is used when you decide to use any genre of writing on any subject.

Note: Pupils are asked to research using the library or the internet. This should be done under the supervision of a teacher, parent or guardian at all times.

Contents

Extract	Skill	Topic	Page
1. Something Nasty in the Lifts	Comprehension	A Little Light Thinking / Deeper Thinking	2
	Vocabulary Work	Wordsearch	3
	Working with Sounds	Suffixes -ant and -ent	3
	Grammar	Capital Letters	4
	Extension Ideas	Chocolate	4
	Writing Genre	Recount Writing	5
2. The New School	Comprehension	A Little Light Thinking / Deeper Thinking	6
	Vocabulary Work	Crossword	7
	Working with Sounds	Silent Letters	7
	Grammar	Punctuation Marks	8
	Extension Ideas	Overcoming Disability	8
	Writing Genre	Recount Writing	9
3. Overcoming Disability to Succeed	Comprehension	A Little Light Thinking / Deeper Thinking	10
	Vocabulary Work	True or False?	11
	Comprehension Work	Cloze Procedure	11
	Working with Words	Words from the Story	12
	Grammar	Capital Letters and Puncuation Marks	12
	Extension Ideas	Famous Songs	13
	Writing Genre	Report Writing	13
4. The Runaway Pram	Comprehension	A Little Light Thinking / Deeper Thinking	14
	Vocabulary Work	Exploring the Word Sorry	15
	Working with Sounds	Suffix -tion	15
	Grammar	Singular and Plural	16
	Extension Ideas	Bull Terrier Dogs	16
	Writing Genre	Report Writing	17
5. The Bear Cub	Comprehension	A Little Light Thinking / Deeper Thinking	18
	Vocabulary Work	Mini Crosswords	19
	Working with Sounds	Suffixes -able and -ible	19
	Grammar	Common and Proper Nouns	20
	Extension Ideas	Investigating Bears	21
	Writing Genre	Explanation Writing	21

Extract	Skill	Topic	Page
6. The Stone Age	Comprehension	A Little Light Thinking Deeper Thinking	22
	Vocabulary Work	What Does it Mean?	23
	Comprehension Work	Cloze Procedure	23
	Word Sort	Group Terms	24
	Grammar	Collective Nouns	24
	Extension Ideas	The Stone Age People	25
	Writing Genre	Explanation Writing	25
7. The Changed World of Matt	Comprehension	A Little Light Thinking Deeper Thinking	26
	Vocabulary Work	Find the Word	27
	Working with Sounds	ie or ei?	27
	Grammar	Personal Pronouns	28
	Extension Ideas	Rip Van Winkle	28
	Writing Genre	Narrative Writing	29
8. Lost in the Jungle	Comprehension	A Little Light Thinking Deeper Thinking	30
	Vocabulary Work	Anagrams	31
	Working with Sounds	Suffixes -ous and -ious	31
	Grammar	Commas	32
	Extension Ideas	Investigating the Amazon Jungle	33
	Writing Genre	Narrative Writing	33
9. Missing from the Skies	Comprehension	A Little Light Thinking Deeper Thinking	34
	Vocabulary Work	Synonyms	35
	Comprehension Work	Cloze Procedure	35
	Word Sort	Thesaurus Work – Descriptive Words	36
	Grammar	Adjectives	36
	Extension Ideas	Presidents of the USA	36
	Writing Genre	Persuasive Writing	37
10. Tilly and the Time Machine	Comprehension	A Little Light Thinking Deeper Thinking	38
	Vocabulary Work	Dictionary Meanings	39
	Working with Sounds	Suffixes -er, -ar and -or	39
	Grammar	Verbs	40
	Extension Ideas	Investigating London	40
	Writing Genre	Persuasive Writing	41

Extract	Skill	Topic	Page
11. Invasion	Comprehension	A Little Light Thinking Deeper Thinking	42
	Vocabulary Work	Alphabetical Order	43
	Working with Sounds	Homophones	43
	Grammar	Adverbs	44
	Extension Ideas	Investigating Anne Frank	45
	Writing Genre	Writing to Socialise	45
12. Amsterdam	Comprehension	A Little Light Thinking Deeper Thinking	46
	Vocabulary Work	Synonyms	47
	Comprehension Work	Cloze Procedure	47
	Working with Words	Dictionary Meanings	48
	Grammar	Apostrophes	48
	Extension Ideas	Vincent van Gogh	48
	Writing Genre	Writing to Socialise	49
13. Monkey Mayhem	Comprehension	A Little Light Thinking Deeper Thinking	50
	Vocabulary Work	Antonyms	51
	Working with Sounds	Suffixes -ic and -ick	51
	Grammar	Compound Words	52
	Extension Ideas	Investigating Zoologists	52
	Writing Genre	Procedural Writing	53
14. Space Above Planet Mars	Comprehension	A Little Light Thinking Deeper Thinking	54
	Vocabulary Work	Jumbled Letters	55
	Working with Sounds	-ough Words	55
	Grammar	Quotation Marks	56
	Extension Ideas	Investigating American States	56
	Writing Genre	Procedural Writing	57
15. Space Exploration	Comprehension	A Little Light Thinking Deeper Thinking	58
	Vocabulary Work	True or False?	59
	Comprehension Work	Cloze Procedure	59
	Word Sort	Prefixes	60
	Grammar	Conjunctions	60
	Extension Ideas	Astronauts	60
	Writing Genre	Free Writing	61

Extract	Skill	Topic	Page
16. The 1,000-Year-Old Boy	Comprehension	A Little Light Thinking Deeper Thinking	62
	Vocabulary Work	Dictionary Work	63
	Working with Sounds	-sion Sound	63
	Grammar	Prepositions	64
	Extension Ideas	Living Long Ago	64
	Writing Genre	Recount Writing	65
17. Parvana's Journey	Comprehension	A Little Light Thinking Deeper Thinking	66
	Vocabulary Work	Synonyms and Antonyms	67
	Working with Sounds	Suffixes -ery, -ory and -ary	67
	Grammar	Similes	68
	Extension Ideas	Investigations	68
	Writing Genre	Recount Writing	69
18. I am Malala	Comprehension	A Little Light Thinking Deeper Thinking	70
	Vocabulary Work	More Synonyms	71
	Comprehension Work	Cloze Procedure	71
	Word Sort	Tired Words – Went	72
	Grammar	Possessive Pronouns	72
	Extension Ideas	Nobel Prizes	73
	Writing Genre	Report Writing	73
19. The Witch Next Door	Comprehension	A Little Light Thinking Deeper Thinking	74
	Vocabulary Work	Word Links	75
	Working with Sounds	Suffix -ture	75
	Grammar	Metaphors	76
	Extension Ideas	Birds	76
	Writing Genre	Report Writing	77
20. Alfie's World	Comprehension	A Little Light Thinking Deeper Thinking	78
	Vocabulary Work	Occupations	79
	Working with Sounds	Suffixes -ence and -ance	79
	Grammar	Contractions	80
	Extension Ideas	The Loch Ness Monster	80
	Writing Genre	Persuasive Writing	81

Extract	Skill	Topic	Page
21. Dramatic Rescues	Comprehension	A Little Light Thinking / Deeper Thinking	82
	Vocabulary Work	Thesaurus Work	83
	Comprehension Work	Cloze Procedure	83
	Word Sort	Proverbs	84
	Grammar	Positive, Comparative and Superlative Degrees of Adjectives	84
	Extension Ideas	Renewable Resources	85
	Writing Genre	Persuasive Writing	85
22. The Television Game Show	Comprehension	A Little Light Thinking / Deeper Thinking	86
	Vocabulary Work	Changing Letter Challenge	87
	Working with Sounds	Root Words	87
	Grammar	Masculine and Feminine Gender	88
	Extension Ideas	Game Shows	88
	Writing Genre	Procedural Writing	89
23. Kidnapped by a Yeti	Comprehension	A Little Light Thinking / Deeper Thinking	90
	Vocabulary Work	Prefixes and Antonyms	91
	Working with Sounds	Rhyming Words Crossword	91
	Grammar	Idioms	92
	Extension Ideas	Mountains	92
	Writing Genre	Procedural Writing	93
24. Unusual Creatures	Comprehension	A Little Light Thinking / Deeper Thinking	94
	Vocabulary Work	True or False?	95
	Comprehension Work	Cloze Procedure	95
	Word Sort	More Tired Words	96
	Grammar	Indirect Speech	96
	Extension Ideas	Creatures in Ireland	97
	Writing Genre	Explanation Writing	97
25. The Boy Detective	Comprehension	A Little Light Thinking / Deeper Thinking	98
	Vocabulary Work	Descriptive Sounds	99
	Working with Sounds	Suffixes -le, -el, -il and -al	99
	Grammar	Abbreviations	100
	Extension Ideas	Detectives	100
	Writing Genre	Explanation Writing	101

Extract		Skill	Topic	Page
26.	**Mahmoud the Refugee**	Comprehension	A Little Light Thinking Deeper Thinking	102
		Vocabulary Work	American Words (Americanisms)	103
		Working with Sounds	Tricky Words Wordsearch	103
		Grammar	Possessive Adjectives	104
		Extension Ideas	Countries	104
		Writing Genre	Writing to Socialise	105
27.	**Syria**	Comprehension	A Little Light Thinking Deeper Thinking	106
		Vocabulary Work	More Synonyms	107
		Comprehension Work	Cloze Procedure	107
		Word Sort	Anagrams	108
		Grammar	Revision of Punctuation Marks	108
		Extension Ideas	Refugees	109
		Writing Genre	Writing to Socialise	109
28.	**Harry Potter Goes to Hogwarts**	Comprehension	A Little Light Thinking Deeper Thinking	110
		Vocabulary Work	Tired Words	111
		Working with Sounds	Homonyms	111
		Grammar	Revision of Speech	112
		Extension Ideas	Harry Potter	112
		Writing Genre	Narrative Writing	113
29.	**The Accident**	Comprehension	A Little Light Thinking Deeper Thinking	114
		Vocabulary Work	Commonly Misspelled Words	115
		Working with Sounds	Suffixes -ful, -some, -ment and -ness	115
		Grammar	Revision of Conjunctions, Prepositions and Contractions	116
		Extension Ideas	Investigations	116
		Writing Genre	Narrative Writing	117
30.	**The Holocaust**	Comprehension	A Little Light Thinking Deeper Thinking	118
		Vocabulary Work	True or False?	119
		Comprehension Work	Cloze Procedure	119
		Working with Sounds	Suffixes -ace, -ade, -ate, -age and -are	120
		Grammar	More Punctuation	120
		Extension Ideas	Hitler and the Nazi Party	121
		Writing Genre	Free Writing	121

Writing Pages   122–152

1

1 Something Nasty in the Lifts

A A Little Light Thinking

1. Where was Mr Wonka when he heard the first scream?
   Mr wonka was in the lobby when he heard the scream

2. What did the *thing* in the lift look like to Mr Wonka?
   It looked like an enormous egg on its pointed end.

3. What did all five shapes in the lifts have in common?
   They were all greenish brown body and red pupil

4. What word did the creatures spell out?
   The creatures spelt out SCRAM.

5. Who ran towards the Great Glass Elevator?
   The people who ran towards the great glass elevator were mr and mrs bucket, charlie, mr wonka, grandpa joe

6. What did Mr Wonka do to make the Great Glass Elevator move?
   Mr wonka undid bolts and pressed buttons

B Deeper Thinking

1. Describe Mr Wonka as he stood gaping at the *thing* in the lift.
   He stood motionless gaping at it his mouth slightly open his eyes stretched as wide as two wheels.

2. How did Charlie know that a second lift was coming down?

3. What sentence tells us that the three lifts opened exactly at the same time?

4. What sentence tells us how frightened Charlie was?

5. When did they all see the word *SCRAM* written?

6. Where did they go when the door to the Great Glass Elevator closed?

CHALLENGE

From where do you think the creatures came? Explain.

ACTIVITIES

C **Vocabulary Work: Wordsearch**

Ring the words from the story in the wordsearch.

t	o	b	b	y	r	m	b	s	d	x	q
p	f	a	i	x	l	l	d	n	k	v	u
t	w	i	s	t	i	n	g	a	m	b	i
u	s	r	c	s	j	k	p	p	z	n	c
y	g	e	i	c	c	h	n	p	v	d	k
d	i	a	r	n	r	r	v	e	c	x	l
d	u	g	p	p	k	e	e	d	m	k	y
o	e	l	y	i	e	l	k	a	x	i	r
f	k	d	q	y	n	n	e	z	m	q	r
q	o	q	t	c	e	g	t	s	h	e	q
a	s	t	i	r	r	e	d	u	a	l	r
g	c	r	e	a	t	u	r	e	e	y	y

scream
quickly
gaping
wrinkles
lobby
stirred
serpent
creature

CHALLENGE
twisting
snapped

D **Working with Sounds: Suffixes -ant and -ent**

Remember: A **suffix** is a group of letters added to other letters to make a word, e.g. -ant and -ent: brilli + ant → brilliant / serp + ent → serpent.

Circle the word that is spelt correctly. Then write it in the space provided.

1. brillant; brilloent; **brilliant;** brillient: _brilliant_
2. **migrant;** migrent; miggrant; miggrent: _migrant_
3. excellant; excelant; **excellent;** excelent: _excellent_
4. servaent; **servant;** serveant; servent: _servent_
5. excitment; excitemant; excitmant; **excitement:** _excitement_
6. presidant; **president;** presadant; presedent: _president_
7. confideent; **confident;** confideant; confadent: _confident_
8. vacent; vacient; vaceint; **vacant:** _vacant_
9. **arguement;** arguemant; argument; argumant: _arguement_
10. plesent; **pleasant;** pleasent; plesant: _pleasant_

3

1 Something Nasty in the Lifts

E Grammar: Capital Letters

Capital letters are used (a) at the start of sentences, (b) for the names of people and places, (c) the pronoun **I**, (d) the main words in the titles of books, plays and films, e.g. *Fantastic Mr Fox* by Roald Dahl, and (e) special days, e.g. Christmas Day.

Write these sentences putting in capital letters where needed.

1. willy wonka stood in the lobby of the space hotel in america.

2. grandma josephine was screaming at charlie and grandpa.

3. danny and i went to see the play *frozen* in london, england.

4. i saw the statue of liberty in new york last year.

5. clara and cian went to see the hurling game in croke park last week.

6. jane read the book *paddington* last august when in spain.

7. our family went to italy to see the leaning tower of piza in july.

8. st stephen's day follows christmas day, every december.

9. sunday, tuesday, thursday and friday are days of the week.

10. paris is the capital city of france.

F Extension Ideas

Use the library or internet to help you with the following exercise.

1. Write four interesting facts about making chocolate.
   (a)
   (b)
   (c)
   (d)

2. Write a few sentences on: (a) If I could own any type of food factory it would be… (b) It would look like…

ACTIVITIES

G Writing Genre: Recount Writing

Grandma Josephine was the first one to notice the strange creature. Write what happened from the point of view of Grandma Josephine. Complete the template below.

Title: _____

Setting: _____

Who is the story about? _____

When did it happen? _____

Where did it happen? _____

What were they doing? _____
_____

Why did it happen? _____
_____

Event 1: _____
_____

Event 2: _____
_____

Event 3: _____
_____

Event 4: _____
_____

Afterwards, how did you feel? _____

Now, use the template to help you recount your story on page 123.

2 The New School

A A Little Light Thinking

1. To where did August and his mother follow Mr Tushman?
   August and his mother followed mr tushman into *his office*

2. Where did August's mother sit in Mr Tushman's office?
   August's mother sat in front of mr tushman's desk.

3. What did August do to stop himself laughing at the painting of Mr Tushman?
   August covered his mouth to keep himself from laughing

4. Which of the three children was the only one not to shake August's hand?
   Charlotte was the only one that didn't shake August's hand.

5. Where did Julian think he should bring August during the tour of the school?
   Julian thought of bringing august to the music room

6. What did Mr Tushman say the music room had a nice selection of?
   Mr tushman said they have a nice selection percussion instruments

B Deeper Thinking

1. What cool stuff did August see on Mr Tushman's desk?
   August really liked the paintings and drawings by students on the wall

2. Why do you think Mr Tushman smiled when August asked if he was called Mr T?

3. Explain why August might have thought that Mr Tushman looked like a pumpkin.

4. How do we know that August was really nervous when he heard the voices outside?

5. Why do you think August felt awkward about a visit to the music room?

6. Explain why you think August might actually enjoy the music room.

CHALLENGE

Write four challenges you think August might face at his new school.
(a)
(b)
(c)
(d)

C Vocabulary Work: Crossword

Complete the crossword to find 10 words from the story.

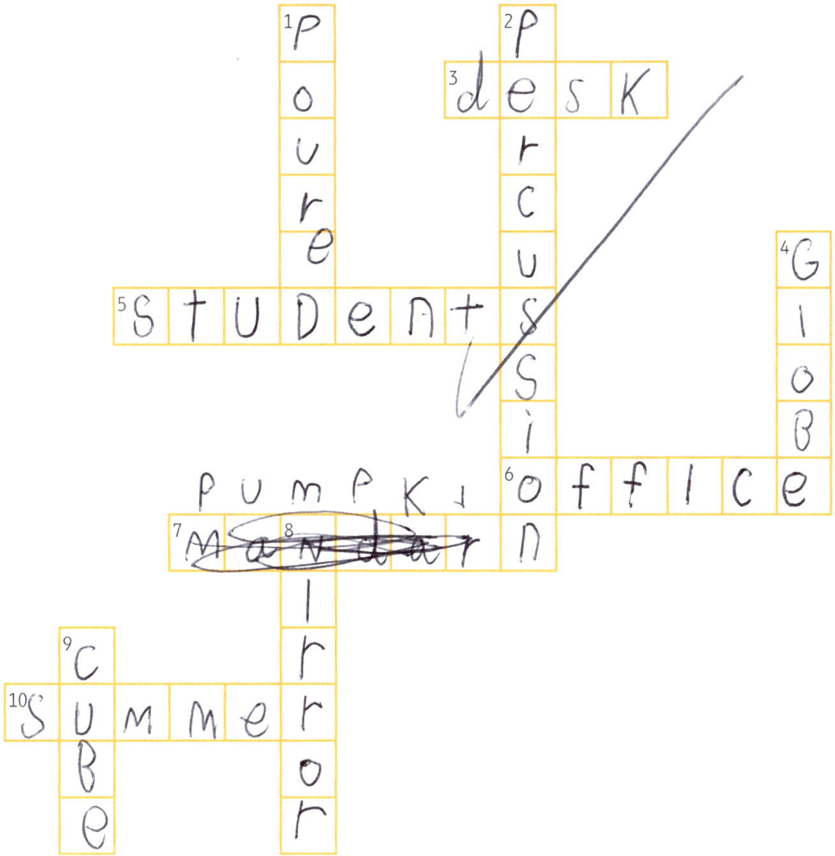

ACROSS

3. A piece of office furniture
5. Scholars/pupils
6. A place of work
7. A large yellow/orange fruit
10. Our hot season

DOWN

1. Flowed/gushed
2. Instruments that are banged
4. A sphere/ball showing the Earth
8. Shows an image or reflection
9. It has six equal square sides

D Working with Sounds: Silent Letters

Remember: Some words contain silent letters – letters we don't sound, e.g. know, school, knit, sword, white, match, etc.

1. Circle the silent letter in the following words.

listen	science	answer	climb	hour
descend	talking	knee	comb	knock

2. Put each word from the word box in a sentence to show its meaning.

(a)

(b)

(c)

(d)

(e)

(f)

(g)

(h)

(i)

(j)

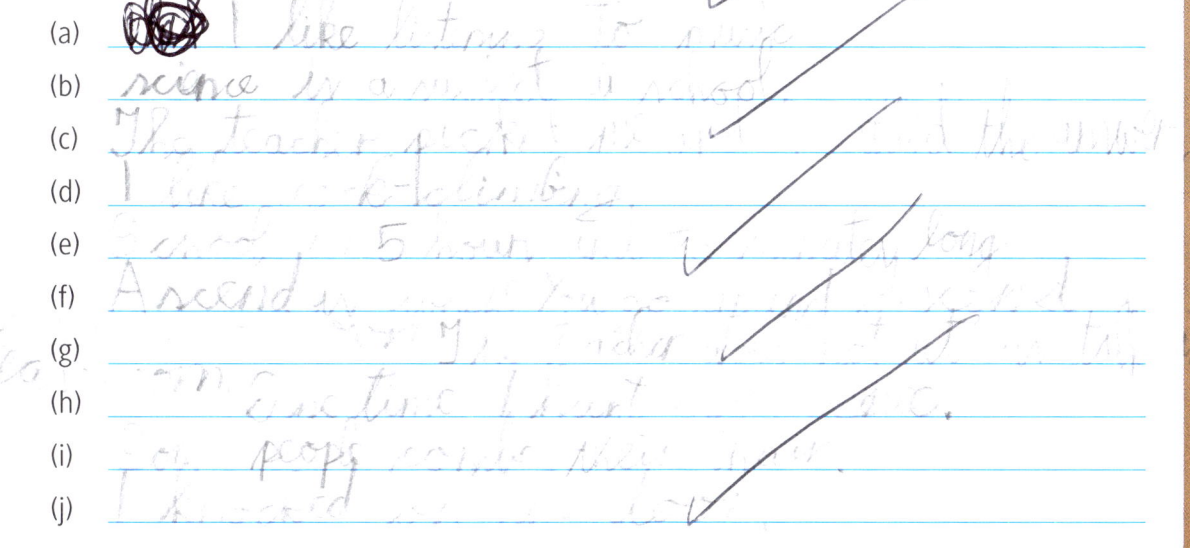

2 The New School

E Grammar: Punctuation Marks

Remember: We must always put either (a) a **question mark** /?/, (b) an **exclamation mark** /!/, or (c) a **full stop** /./ at the end of a sentence or where there is a question or an exclamation.

(a) A **question mark** is used after a question is asked, e.g. Who kicked the ball**?**
(b) An **exclamation mark** is used to show surprise, joy or anger. It is like writing in a loud voice, e.g. 'Catch it**!**' said the girl loudly.
(c) Otherwise, a **full stop** is used at the end of a sentence**.**

Write the following sentences using the correct punctuation marks.

1. 'No' I answered, though I was thinking yes

2. 'My mom and dad had a teacher called Miss Butt,' I said

3. 'Is that a pumpkin' I said, pointing to the framed painting

4. In what year did the Vikings come to Ireland

5. 'Get off that wall' shouted the neighbour to the children

6. Is it possible that Cian will score the winning goal in the game

7. 'Would all the children in red coats please sit down?' asked teacher

8. What's wrong with you Will you please listen to the question

9. Don't be silly Can't you see that I'm going to give the book back to you

10. What a beautiful day exclaimed the holiday maker in July

F Extension Ideas

Use the library or internet to help you with the following exercise.

1. List six people with a disability who have succeeded in life despite their disability.
   (a) _____ (b) _____
   (c) _____ (d) _____
   (e) _____ (f) _____

2. Write three difficulties a blind person might encounter during a normal day.
   (a) _____
   (b) _____
   (c) _____

ACTIVITIES

G Writing Genre: Recount Writing

Mrs Garcia, the school secretary, had a bird's eye view of all that happened that day in Mr Tushman's office. Write her eyewitness account of the day August visited the school. Complete the template below.

Title: A suprise visit

Setting: beecher prep middle school

Who is the story about? August

When did it happen? Summer holidays

Where did it happen? mr tushmans office

What were they doing? August and his mum were taking a look around

Why did it happen? because its augusts first school

Event 1: I had a good feeling about August from the start

Event 2: And then he went into mr tushmans office

Event 3: and when he went out of there I thought he could make some friends

Event 4: although he was a bit overwhelmed he got through

Afterwards, how did you feel? I think hes gonna be a great student

Now, use the template to help you recount your story on page 124.

3 Overcoming Disability to Succeed

A A Little Light Thinking

1. Where was Helen Keller born? *Alabama in the state*
2. What is Braille? *Braille is a language for the blind* ~~scribbled out~~
3. Name the wife of Franklin D. Roosevelt. *Eleanor*
4. What name was given to the worst economic crash in history? *The great deppresion*
5. What age was Stevie Wonder when he released his first album? *Stevie releared his first album, when he was 12*
6. What disease did Stephen Hawking develop? *Stephen*
7. What are needed to view black holes properly? _____
8. Name the book written by Stephen Hawking. _____

B Deeper Thinking

1. Why do you think it was such an achievement for Helen Keller to read using Braille and to use a typewriter?

2. Why do you think Franklin D. Roosevelt was home-schooled?

3. Why do you think Franklin D. Roosevelt was elected President of the USA?

4. Do you think the stage name *Stevie Wonder* sounds better than his original name? Why?

5. Why could Stephen Hawking be described as a *miracle man*?

CHALLENGE

How might the achievements of these people help others who have a disability?

C. Vocabulary Work: True or False?

Write true or false after each statement.

1. Helen Keller was born in 1840. — false
2. Helen was around 18 months old when she got sick. — true
3. Helen wrote more than 10 books before she died. — true
4. Franklin D. Roosevelt had one brother. — false
5. Roosevelt promised a *New Deal* that would give Canadians a better life. — false
6. Roosevelt was president right up until his death in 1945. — true
7. Stevie Wonder was born five weeks premature. — false
8. Stevie Wonder has recorded songs with many different stars. — true
9. Stephen Hawking was born in Scotland. — false
10. Stephen Hawking died at the age of 77. — false

D. Comprehension Work: Cloze Procedure

Complete the story using words from the word box.

disability	Braille	Roosevelt	President	people	elected
eyesight	bumps	polio	smell	diagnosed	motor
blinded	crutches	incubator	communicate	involved	young

Against All Odds

Many **people** have overcome a **disability** to become famous in different fields. Helen Keller became very ill when she was very **young** and lost both her **eyesight** and hearing. Anne Sullivan taught her **Braille** which is a special reading system where the letters are tiny **bumps** on a page.

Franklin Delano **Roosevelt** became ill with **polio** when he was 39 years old. To get around, he had to use **crutches** or a wheelchair. In 1932, he became **President** of the USA. He has the unique distinction of being the only President of the USA to have been **elected** four times.

Stevie Wonder was **blinded** when accidentally given too much oxygen in his hospital **incubator** when he was just a baby. Later in his life, he was **involved** in a traffic accident where he lost both his sense of **smell** and taste.

Stephen Hawking had a normal childhood. However, at the age of 22 he was **diagnosed** with a rare form of **motor** neurone disease. He had a special computerised voice box made which he used to **communicate** with the outside world.

3 Overcoming Disability to Succeed language

E Working with Words: Words from the Story

1. Complete the following sentences to show the meaning of the underlined words.
   (a) Stephen Hawking communicated _with a computerized with people_ ✗ *without talking*
   (b) He was diagnosed _____
   (c) Braille is _____ ✗
   (d) A wheelchair is _a chair with wheels for people without who_ ✗ *can't walk*
   (e) An incubator is a _____ ✗

2. Use the clues to find the words from the story.
   (a) victory: t r i u m p h ✓
   (b) not sick: h e a l t h y
   (c) very rich: w e a l t h y ✓
   (d) head of a country: p r e s i d e n t
   (e) set of songs: a l b u m   *Prompted*
   (f) well known: f a m o u s
   (g) twelve in a year: M o N T h S
   (h) not on purpose: a c c i d e n t
   (i) agreed to: p r o m o t e d
   (j) to be voted in: e l e c t e d
   (k) mouth organ: h a r m o n i c a
   (l) the Earth's pull: _ r _ v _ t _

3. Write a clue for each of the following words.
   (a) college: _____
   (b) disease: _____
   (c) doctor: _____

F Grammar: Capital Letters and Punctuation Marks

Rewrite these sentences putting in capital letters and punctuation marks where needed.

1. 'are you going to rome next summer,' inquired the nosey boy
   "Are you going to Rome next summer;"

2. jane went to kerry in ireland on her holidays
   _____

3. simona and cian both like reading books by jacqueline wilson
   _____

4. 'stand well back,' said the guard in dublin
   _____

5. daniel radcliffe was an actor in the *harry potter* films
   _____

6. rowan played football with clara in the park on Sunday
   _____

G **Extension Ideas**

Use the library or internet to help you with the following exercise.
Choose the correct word from the word box to complete the titles of these famous songs.

    Rhapsody   *Stone*   *Always*   *Dancing*   *Time*

(a) *Baby One More* _____ *by Britney Spears.*

(b) *Bohemian* _____ *by Queen.*

(c) *Like a Rolling* _____ *by Bob Dylan.*

(d) *I Will* _____ *Love You by Whitney Houston.*

(e) _____ *Queen by ABBA.*

H **Writing Genre: Report Writing**

Michael J. Fox is a famous Canadian-American actor and comedian who was diagnosed with Parkinson's Disease in 1991 at the age of 29. Research, plan and write a report on Michael J. Fox using the following template.

Title: _____

What does he do? _____

Where does he live? _____

Description (personal details): _____

What significant things is he famous for? _____

_____

What disability does he have? _____

How does it affect him? _____

What has he accomplished? _____

_____

Summarising comment: _____

_____

_____

Now, use the template to help you write your report on page 125.

4 The Runaway Pram

A A Little Light Thinking

1. What was in the garbage bag that they found with the pram?
   (a) baby clothes   (b) toys

2. Where is house number 21 situated?
   Number 21 is situated at the bottom of the hill

3. What does Andy first try to use as a brake to stop the pram?
   A Porky Pig Rattle

4. What house number does the bull terrier live at? Number 19

5. What did Andy pull out of the bag of baby gear? A plastic bottle

6. What word meaning *crossroads* is in the text? ___

7. What happened when the bottle of baby powder hit the ground?
   The baby powder exploded into a cloud

8. From where was the sound of bells coming? The sound of bells came from behind

Andy

B Deeper Thinking

1. Why do you think the pram was put on the rubbish pile?
   _____
   _____

2. Do you think Andy was clever to trust Danny with the pram? Explain.
   _____
   _____

3. Why do you think the traffic stopped when the doll landed on the road?
   _____
   _____

4. How do you think Andy felt when the pram got stuck on the train tracks?
   _____
   _____

5. What three words best describe Andy?
   (a) _____ (b) _____ (c) _____

6. Was Andy right not to think of the dog after he got over the train tracks? Explain.
   _____
   _____

CHALLENGE

What do you think would be the best way to stop the runaway pram?
_____
_____
_____

ACTIVITIES

C Vocabulary Work: Exploring the Word Sorry

Andy uses the word **sorry** in two different ways during the story.
(a) *You'll be sorry!*: Here the word **sorry** is used as a threat.
(b) *Sorry about this*: Here, **sorry** is used to show remorse for doing something wrong.

Match the following sorry statements with their meanings.

you'll be sorry	I regret asking the question
sorry for your troubles	regretfully or unfortunately
sorry state of affairs	to make a threat
feeling sorry for yourself	having empathy for another person
sorry I asked	something unpleasant to look at
sorry to say	to be in an unfortunate situation
better to be safe than sorry	to be focused on your own unhappiness
a sorry sight	better to be cautious than regret it

D Working with Sounds: Suffix -tion

Words ending with the suffix **-tion** have a /**shun**/ sound, e.g. intersec**tion**, collec**tion**, etc.

1. **Put the following -tion words from the word box in the correct sentences below.**

   ~~station~~   ~~subtraction~~   ~~description~~   ~~caution~~   ~~reflection~~
   ~~fraction~~   ~~reception~~   invention   ~~question~~   ~~election~~

   (a) The witness gave a detailed _description_ of the thief to the Garda.
   (b) Take away and minus are other words for _subtraction_.
   (c) The girl put up her hand to ask the teacher a _question_.
   (d) The people voted in the general _election_ that was called last year.
   (e) The train slowed down as it approached the _station_ in the city.
   (f) The _caution_ of the wheel changed transportation for the better.
   (g) He could see his _reflection_ as he looked into the water.
   (h) Teacher asked us to get a _fraction_ of the whole number.
   (i) The army used great _invention_ when examining the suspicious package.
   (j) The family checked in at the _reception_ desk in the hotel.

2. **Put the following -tion words in sentences of your own to show their meaning.**

   (a) population: In 2022 the population of Ireland was 5000
   (b) selection: I had a selection of option
   (c) multiplication: I don't like multiplication
   (d) conversation: They had a conversation.
   (e) destination: People got on a journey to get to the destination
   (f) examination: The doctor examinated a patient
   (g) decoration: People put up decoration for traditional holidays

4 The Runaway Pram

E Grammar: Singular and Plural

Singular means one, e.g. pram. **Plural** means more than one, e.g. prams.

(a) Most words simply require the addition of **s** to make them plural, e.g. bag → bag**s**.

(b) For words ending in a consonant followed by the letter **y**, change the **y** to **ies**,
e.g. fl**y** → fl**ies** / sp**y** → sp**ies** / apiar**y** → apiar**ies**

(c) For words ending in a vowel followed by the letter **y**, add **s**, e.g. monk**ey** → monk**eys**.

(d) For words ending in the letters **o**, **s**, **x**, **ch** or **sh**, add **es**, e.g. match → match**es**.

(e) Some words change completely, e.g. tooth → teeth / foot → feet / child → children.

Rewrite these sentences putting all the nouns (naming words) into plural form.

1. The man caught the burglar as he entered the house.
   The men caught the burglars as they entered the houses.

2. The lady saw the fox running in the field near the tree.
   The ladies saw the foxes running in the fields near the trees.

3. The fly ate the spider that it trapped in the web in the corner.
   The flies ate the spiders that it trapped in the webs in the corners.

4. The child broke the brush in the garden that was beside the stream.
   The children broke the brushes in the gardens that was beside the streams.

5. The family ate the potato that was boiled in the pot on the cooker.
   The families ate the potatoes that was boiled in the pots in the cookers.

6. The monkey sat in the tree in the middle of the forest.
   The monkeys sat in the trees in the middle of the forests.

7. The baby cried in the church at the bottom of the mountain.
   The babies cried in the churches at the bottom of the mountains.

8. The hero spoke to the crowd as she returned from the battle.
   The heroes spoke to the crowds as she returned from the battles.

F Extension Ideas

Use the library or internet to help you with the following exercise.

Write four facts about bull terrier dogs. (a) What do they look like? (b) Are they big or small? (c) Do they make good pets? (d) Are they good guard dogs? Explain.

(a) _____

(b) _____

(c) _____

(d) _____

ACTIVITIES

G **Writing Genre: Report Writing**

Imagine that Mr Broadbent went to the Garda station to report the incident of Andy in the runaway pram. You are the Garda on duty. Write the report you would have taken from Mr Broadbent using the title: *Report on a runaway pram*. Complete the template below.

Title: **Report on a runaway pram**

What did he see? _____

Where did he see it? _____

Description 1: What did the boy look like? _____
_____

Description 2: What did the pram look like? _____
_____

Where was he going? _____

Who was with him? _____

When did this happen? _____

Summarising comment: _____
_____

Now, use the template to help you write a report on page 126.

5 The Bear Cub

A A Little Light Thinking

1. Who answered Jo when he called for Rouf? *the crows*
2. Where was the brown smattering of blood? *on a tree*
3. What did he call out as he clambered over fallen trees? *He was calling for Rouf*
4. What was sitting in the mouth of the small cave? *a bear cub*
5. Where was the man standing? *The man was N*
6. What was the bear cub doing as it ventured out of the cave? *The cub was coming to the man*
7. What was the man holding in his hands? *he was holding*
8. What reason did the man give as to why he wanted to get home?

B Deeper Thinking

1. What reason might the villagers have for killing the bear?

2. What words tell us that the boy was crying?

3. Why do you think the bear cub was waving one of its front paws at Rouf?

4. Why do you think Rouf swung round with his *hackles* up?

5. Who was the *little fellow*?

6. Why do you think the bear cub couldn't resist the milk?

CHALLENGE

Explain what you think the mother bear did to save her cub.

C Vocabulary Work: Mini Crosswords

Read the clues to fill in the blank spaces. Each word is a noun.

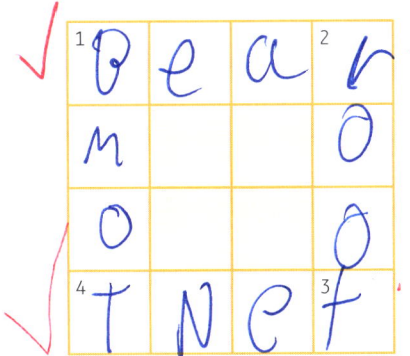

¹B	e	a	²r
m			o
o			o
⁴t	N	³e	f

1. Big hairy animal killed in the story →
2. The part of a plant in the ground ↓
3. What you sleep in while camping ←
4. Another word for a grave ↑

¹m	i	l	²k
r			i
a			N
⁴f	l	³o	G

1. A liquid poured on cereal →
2. _king_ and queen ↓
3. Game played with clubs ←
4. Animals are reared here by a farmer ↑

D Working with Sounds: Suffixes -able and -ible

Sometimes, it is difficult to know if a word ends with the suffix -able or -ible, e.g. cap**able** / invis**ible**. The suffix -able is attached to complete root words (enjoy + able) while -ible is connected to incomplete root words. There are exceptions!

Add the correct ending and put each word in the correct sentence.

(a) comfort**able** (b) suit**ible** (c) sens**ible** (d) respons**ible** (e) port**able**
(f) poss**ible** (g) fashion**ible** (h) horr**ible** (i) vis**able** (j) avail**able**

1. There were no rooms _available_ in the hotel because of the concert.
2. 'How was it _possible_ for you to solve the equation so quickly?' she asked.
3. A mobile phone is a _portable_ device because you carry it with you.
4. I bought the couch because it was very _comfortable_ to sit on.
5. The mountain was not _visible_ due to a blanket of fog.
6. 'We don't think that film is _suitable_ for young children,' said Dad.
7. The _responsible_ girl was made prefect of her class.
8. The man bought the suit as it was trendy and _fashionable_.
9. 'Is it really a _horrible_ thing to vandalise a life buoy?' asked the lady.
10. The rain poured down, so they had a _sensible_ day in the park.

5 The Bear Cub

E Grammar: Common and Proper Nouns

A **common noun** is the name of a person, place, animal or thing,
e.g. boy, shop, dog, table, etc.
A **proper noun** is the name of a **particular** person, place, animal or thing,
e.g. Sofia, Cork, Frankie the dog, O'Neill's footballs, etc.
Proper nouns always have a capital letter.

1. Underline all the nouns in the following sentences. Only write the *proper nouns*.

   (a) Barcelona is a city in Spain. (i) *Barcelona* (ii) *Spain*
   (b) Mary is going to the cinema with Jane. (i) *Mary* (ii) *Jane*
   (c) Sarah, my cousin, lives in Belfast. (i) *Belfast* (ii) *Sarah*
   (d) My sister, Sofia, has a dog called Bella. (i) *Sofia* (ii) *Bella*
   (e) Chris put the book on the table. (i) *Chris* (ii) ~~~~
   (f) We ate fish and chips for dinner. (i) _____ (ii) _____
   (g) Emily ran a marathon in Boston. (i) *Boston* (ii) *Emily*
   (h) The ship hit rocks near the coastline. (i) _____ (ii) _____
   (i) The floor is made of wood. (i) _____ (ii) _____
   (j) The king lived in the palace with his son. (i) _____ (ii) _____

2. Write four of your own nouns under the following headings.

Noun	Person	Place
common	(a)	(a)
proper	(b)	(b)
common	(c)	(c)
proper	(d)	(d)

Noun	Animal	Thing
common	(a)	(a)
proper	(b)	(b)
common	(c)	(c)
proper	(d)	(d)

F Extension Ideas

Use the library or internet to help you with the following exercise.

1. Find out as much as you can about bears under the following headings.

    (a) They live in _____

    (b) They eat _____

    (c) There are _____ types _____

    (d) They are _____

2. What wild baby animal would you like as a pet? _____

    (a) Where would you find it? _____

    (b) Where would you keep it? _____

    (c) What would you feed it? _____

G Writing Genre: Explanation Writing

The people in Jo's village killed a bear. People hunt and kill animals for many reasons such as food and clothes. As a result, many animals have become extinct.
Research and write an explanation as to why some animals have become extinct.

Title: **Why some animals have become extinct**

Definition: What is it? _____

How does it happen? _____

Where does it happen? _____

When does it happen? _____

Why does it happen? _____

What animals are extinct? _____

Are there any animals nearly extinct? _____

Special features: Are there any laws to protect this from happening? _____

_____

_____

Now, use the template to write your explanation on page 127.

6 The Stone Age

A A Little Light Thinking

1. What did the Stone Age people make using stone?
   stones.

2. Why did the early Stone Age people keep moving from place to place?
   Maybe it is because they are nomads.

3. From where did they get water?
   They got water from streams lakes and rivers.

4. Explain how Stone Age people made fire.
   They rubbed 2 pieces of flint together.

5. What was *ochre*?
   They would cover up the cave entrance with

6. For what did they use the skins of animals?
   They made it into shoes and clothes

B Deeper Thinking

1. Why do you think that the Stone Age people chose to live in caves?

2. Why do you think the wooden and stone tools and weapons were a disadvantage to them?
   Probably

3. Why do you think catching fish with their hands was so difficult?

4. Why was fire so important to the Stone Age people?
   Well it's probably

5. Give three reasons why cows were very useful to the Stone Age people.
   (a)
   (b)
   (c)

6. How do you think the Bronze Age improved life for the people after the Stone Age?

CHALLENGE

Explain how you think friction works to make fire.

ACTIVITIES

C Vocabulary Work: What Does it Mean?

Complete the following sentences to show the meaning of the underlined word.

1. The nomads *travelled from place to place.*
2. They used hammerstones *I don't know.*
3. They made more sophisticated *objects for the fishing.*
4. They used friction *to light the fire.*
5. They often used camouflage *to stay hidden.*
6. Ochre was used *for cave paintings.*
7. The wooden plough *was put ~~~~ behind the cow.*
8. Bronze was *~~ copper and tin put together.*
9. Their settlements *were good.* ✗ not good enough
10. Our ancestors *~ were in the stone age.*

D Comprehension Work: Cloze Procedure

Complete the story by filling in the blanks using the words from the word box.

~~streams~~	~~hammerstones~~	grass	hides	twigs
~~nomads~~	~~live~~	~~cook~~	decorated	~~animals~~
~~flint~~	~~search~~	Stone	fire	~~camouflage~~
~~heat~~	~~spears~~	~~hunter~~	hands	discover

The Stone Age

During the *Stone* Age, the people were *hunter*-gatherers. They were called *nomads* as they had to wander from place to place in *search* of food. They dug large holes in the ground to trap wild *animals*. They covered the holes with sticks and *twigs/grass* so that the animals would not be frightened away. They then used rough *spears* ~~hammerstones~~ to kill some of the animals. They ate the meat of the animals and used the _____ to make clothes and shoes. They caught fish in the *stream*, rivers and lakes. At first, they caught fish using their bare *hands* but later, they used long, wooden *spears* to catch them.

They were the first people to *discover* how to make fire. They did this by rubbing two pieces of *flint* together to make a spark. This spark then lit the dry ~~grass~~ and leaves. They used fire for a variety of reasons. It gave them *heat* during the long, cold, winter nights. It also frightened away the many wild animals that attacked them. They were now able to *cook* their food which was much better for their health.

The caves the Stone Age people lived in were very basic. They would often *camoflauge* the entrance using rocks or sticks. They *decorated* the walls of their caves with handprints and animal drawings. They wouldn't have considered these caves as homes. It was only when they discovered how to make *fire* that they began to *live* in the caves.

23

6 The Stone Age

E Word Sort: Group Terms

1. Write one name for each of these groups, e.g. terrier, greyhound, labrador = dogs.

(a)	carrot, cabbage, turnip, parsnip	tomato ✗
(b)	plum, apple, pear, banana	orange ✗
(c)	lorry, car, bus, train	ferry ✗
(d)	alligator, lizard, crocodile, snake	chamelon ✗
(e)	beech, ash, oak, horse chestnut	blossom ✗
(f)	soccer, golf, basketball, swimming	Boxing ✗
(g)	crow, magpie, pigeon, robin	tit ✗
(h)	plaice, trout, salmon, cod	hake ✗
(i)	bull, ram, boar, stallion	✗
(j)	Dublin, Galway, Cork, Belfast	Kilkenny ✗

2. Write four words that go in each of the following groups.

(a) flowers: (i) dandelion (ii) lavender
           (iii) ✗   (iv) ✗

(b) countries: (i) america (ii) scotland
            (iii) wales   (iv) england

F Grammar: Collective Nouns

A **collective noun** is the name given to a collection of people or things, e.g. a **herd** of cattle.

Write the correct collective noun for the following using words from the word box.

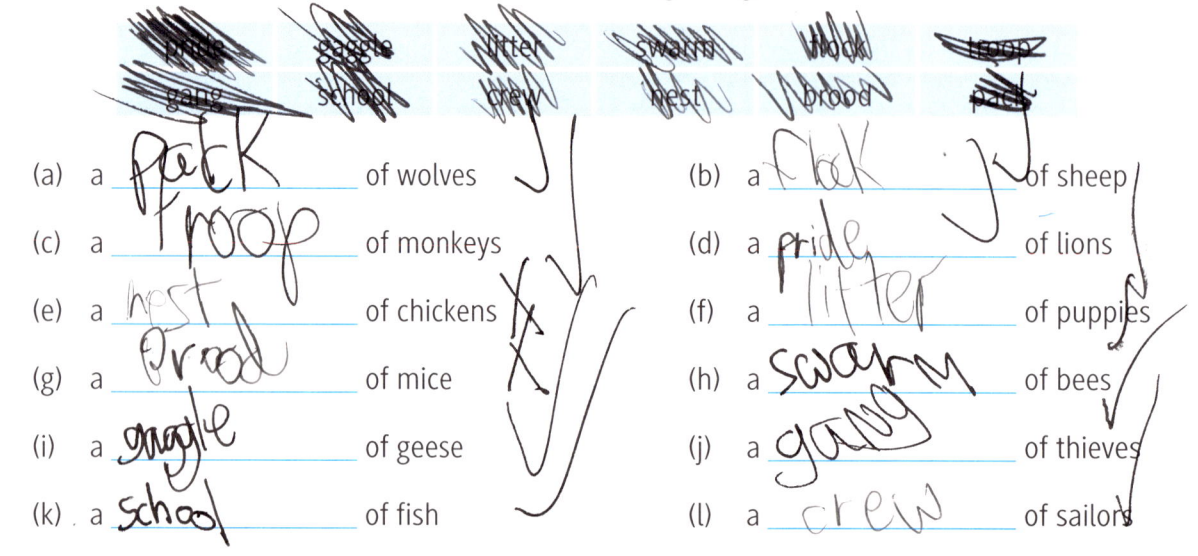

~~pride   gaggle   litter   swarm   flock   troop~~
~~gang   school   crew   nest   brood   pack~~

(a) a **pack** of wolves   (b) a **flock** of sheep
(c) a **troop** of monkeys   (d) a **pride** of lions
(e) a **nest** of chickens   (f) a **litter** of puppies
(g) a **brood** of mice   (h) a **swarm** of bees
(i) a **gaggle** of geese   (j) a **gang** of thieves
(k) a **school** of fish   (l) a **crew** of sailors

G Extension Ideas

Use the headings in the table to write what you have learned about the Stone Age people.

What they ate	Tools they used	Clothes they wore	Where they lived

H Writing Genre: Explanation Writing

The Stone Age people were the first people to discover fire. Write an explanation as to why the Stone Age people needed fire. Complete the template below.

Title: **Why the Stone Age people needed fire**

Definition: What is it? _____

How did they make it? _____

Where did they get the materials they needed? _____

When did they need it? _____

Why was it so important? _____

What did they use it for? _____

How did it make life easier for them? _____

Special features: What are the dangers of fire? _____

_____
_____
_____

Now, use the template to write your explanation on page 128.

25

7 The Changed World of Matt

A A Little Light Thinking

1. What age was Matt at the start of the story? _____
2. What was the first thing Matt noticed when he woke up? _____
3. How much taller was he than the day before? _____
4. What was covered in blond fuzz? _____
5. What was Matt's mum doing when he came downstairs? _____
6. What were Pam and Greg munching? _____
7. What was the name of the family dog? _____
8. What was the name of Matt's school? _____

B Deeper Thinking

1. How do you think Matt felt when he saw his feet?
   _____
   _____

2. What sort of relationship do you think Matt had with his siblings? Explain.
   _____
   _____

3. Explain why Matt thought the doorknob was in the wrong place.
   _____
   _____

4. Why do you think that nobody jumped to help Matt when he fell down the stairs?
   _____
   _____

5. Why do you think Matt's mum was getting so impatient?
   _____
   _____

6. Why do you think Matt was not ready for high school?
   _____
   _____

CHALLENGE

Do you think Matt will have a good day at school? Explain.

_____
_____
_____

C **Vocabulary Work: Find the Word**

1. Write four words for each column that include the letters of the given words.

sat	age	lip	old	late	fit
e.g. satin	e.g. stage	e.g. slipway	e.g. golden	e.g. slate	e.g. fitness

2. Write the shorter word that is in each of the following words.

   (a) covers _____ (b) brush _____ (c) little _____
   (d) chat _____ (e) shut _____ (f) race _____
   (g) aware _____ (h) clothes _____ (i) growl _____
   (j) scold _____ (k) better _____ (l) course _____

D **Working with Sounds: ie or ei?**

The general rule is that **i** comes before **e** except after **c**, e.g. bel**ie**f, fr**ie**nd, etc. If the word has a **long /ee/** sound, the letter **c** is often followed by **ei**, e.g. c**ei**ling, rec**ei**ve, etc.
However, there are many exceptions to this rule, e.g. s**cie**nce, so**cie**ty, gla**cie**r, an**cie**nt, etc.

Rewrite the following using a word from the word box for each underlined word.

receive	ceiling	shrieked	field
thief	piece	yield	conceited

1. The <u>burglar</u> stole the jewellery from the house in the country.
   _____

2. The farmer was cutting the <u>meadow</u> with a tractor.
   _____

3. I had to <u>stop</u> quickly at the junction in the road.
   _____

4. Dad gave the child a <u>portion</u> of the birthday cake.
   _____

5. There was a crack in the <u>top section</u> of the room.
   _____

6. The boy <u>screamed</u> when he heard the noise.
   _____

7. I was hoping to <u>get</u> a nice present in the post from my parents.
   _____

8. The <u>big-headed</u> footballer was not admired by any of the team's fans.
   _____

7 The Changed World of Matt

E Grammar: Personal Pronouns

A **personal pronoun** is a word that takes the place of a noun. The personal pronouns are as follows: **I, you, he, she, it, we, they, me, us, her, him, them**.

1. Write a suitable personal pronoun to complete the following sentences.
   - (a) '_____ couldn't stop staring at myself,' said Matt.
   - (b) He saw his lip. _____ was covered in blond fuzz.
   - (c) Cian went to the film but _____ was bored by it.
   - (d) Mam looked under the table but _____ could not find her phone.
   - (e) Sam and Sue went to town and _____ bought some presents.
   - (f) '_____ will make us late for school,' said Pam to Matt.
   - (g) 'I hope _____ all get to go on holiday this year,' said Mum.
   - (h) The lifeguard tried to save the swimmer, but _____ was in vain.
   - (i) _____ all walked down the path to wait at the bus stop.
   - (j) If _____ work hard you should definitely succeed.

2. Use the correct personal pronouns in the sentences.
   Read the information in the brackets to help you.
   - (a) _____ is dreaming. (Jane)
   - (b) _____ are going to Dublin. (my mother and I)
   - (c) _____ is playing football in the park. (Tom)
   - (d) _____ is barking in the back garden. (the dog)
   - (e) _____ are hanging in the wardrobe. (the coats)
   - (f) _____ is red and looks great in the sun! (the car)
   - (g) _____ are in the forest. (the trees)
   - (h) _____ are watching television in the sitting room. (the children)
   - (i) _____ likes swimming at the weekend. (Rachel)
   - (j) _____ gave John a present for his birthday. (Claire and I)

F Extension Ideas

Use the library or internet to help you with the following exercise.
Who was Rip Van Winkle? Write about what happened to him.

ACTIVITIES

G **Writing Genre: Narrative Writing**

Matt wakes up one morning to find he is four years older than he was the night before. Imagine you woke up one morning to find that you were five years older.

(a) What would you look like? (b) How would you act? (c) What would you wear?

Plan and write your story.

I look like…	
I wear…	
I like to…	
Behaviour: Good or bad?	
I say…	

Now, use the template to write your story on page 129.

29

8 Lost in the Jungle

A A Little Light Thinking

1. Where was the little aeroplane when Fred saw it?
   The aeroplane was in the trees

2. What did the singed hair on his arm smell like? eggy

3. What did Fred do when he heard the voice for the first time?
   He hurled animal dung at them.

4. What words did Fred hear from behind the second bush?
   For god's sake, don't throw things

5. What colour was the girl's hair? The girl's hair was blonde

6. What was the blonde girl's name? Con/Constantia

7. What was about three inches from Fred's shoes?
   A snake was beside Fred's shoes

8. Describe the snake.
   The snake was speckled brown and black and its head was as big as a fist

B Deeper Thinking

1. Why do you think Fred wondered if he was dead?
   It was because Fred thought that if he was dead at least it would be quiet

2. How do you think Fred felt when he heard the voice? Explain.
   Terrified, Shocked but also kind of relieved that he found another person.

3. What sort of girl do you think Constantia is? Use words from the story.
   Aggressive, stubborn and a bit mean.

4. Why do you think the young boy wouldn't talk?
   He was to shocked to the point where he was breathless and couldn't talk

5. How do you think Fred felt when the second bush parted?
   When the second bush parted Fred's heart took a great leap.

6. Do you think the children were brave? Explain.
   I think the children were very brave because they survived a snake 3 inches away from some one.

CHALLENGE

What do you think the children should do now?
Explore around the forest to figure out what to do next

C Vocabulary Work: Anagrams

An **anagram** is made by using the letters of a word in a different order to make a new word, e.g. spat → taps / listen → silent / shaded → dashed / leader → dealer.

Use the clues to write the anagrams for the following words.

(a)	death	to have really disliked someone	hated
(b)	sent	items used to catch fish	nets
(c)	rose	something painful	sore
(d)	chin	a unit of measurement (no longer used)	inch
(e)	trees	to manoeuvre a vehicle	steer
(f)	shriek	people who trek up hills	hikers
(g)	arms	male sheep	rams
(h)	parted	to leave	depart
(i)	leap	light in colour or shade	pale
(j)	earth	circulates your blood	heart

D Working with Sounds: Suffixes -ous and -ious

The **-ous** suffix has an /us/ sound, e.g. nerv**ous**, fam**ous**, jeal**ous**.
With words ending in **-ious** the **i** has a /y/ sound e.g. obv**ious**, cur**ious**, ser**ious**.
Find the 10 -ous and -ious words in the wordsearch.

Find the 10 -ous or -ious words in the wordsearch.

d	m	e	e	i	a	o	i	l	d	u	o	k	m	r
l	r	s	u	o	i	r	e	t	s	y	m	f	j	i
s	n	u	m	e	r	o	u	s	l	f	a	g	b	a
a	l	o	m	j	x	f	s	q	p	t	s	z	t	n
s	r	i	t	z	x	o	d	n	w	j	u	u	n	n
t	v	r	f	t	o	s	a	s	t	r	o	u	s	o
r	a	a	f	j	q	v	h	n	y	t	m	r	i	b
o	r	l	q	s	g	n	g	n	b	d	r	j	c	v
u	i	i	b	j	s	y	e	c	n	e	o	e	g	i
s	o	h	h	q	f	u	r	v	d	v	n	a	c	o
w	u	i	x	s	v	y	o	v	s	h	e	l	q	u
i	s	g	m	b	r	f	u	v	g	t	z	o	q	s
e	p	v	e	n	b	u	s	s	r	a	j	u	f	r
n	r	y	j	q	x	r	d	u	i	e	i	s	u	l
o	t	l	q	r	x	n	o	f	h	z	n	z	p	y

mysterious
obvious
various
numerous
jealous
disastrous
nervous
hilarious
enormous
dangerous

8 Lost in the Jungle

E Grammar: Commas

A **comma** /,/ is used to separate adjectives in any type of list. The last adjective does not need a comma after it, e.g. She walked into the wide, bright, spacious room.
A comma is also used to separate nouns in a list. The noun before **and** does not need a comma after it, e.g. I study geography, history, maths and science at school.

1. Rewrite the following sentences inserting commas in the correct places.

   (a) I saw cows chickens lambs and pigs on the farm.
   I saw cows, chickens, lambs and pigs on the farm

   (b) The girl bought bread milk cheese and butter in the supermarket.
   The girl bought bread, milk, cheese and butter in the supermarket

   (c) I walked down the long dark narrow and frightening street.
   I walked down the long, dark, narrow road

   (d) I saw cars lorries bicycles and jeeps on the road.
   I saw cars, lorries, bicycles and jeeps on the road

   (e) 'Did you buy shoes socks runners and trousers in the shop?' asked Mum.
   'Did you buy shoes, socks, runners and trousers in the shop?' asked Mum

   (f) The room was warm bright cosy and comfortable.
   The room was warm, bright, cosy and comfortable

   (g) The burglar snatched jewellery money phones and computers from the house.
   The burglar snatched jewellery, money, phones and computers from the house

   (h) I went to London Paris Berlin and Madrid on holidays.
   I went to London, Paris, Berlin and Madrid on holidays

2. Below are sets of sentences. Turn each set into one sentence using commas, e.g. I bought milk in the shop. I also bought grapes. I also bought bread.
   → I bought milk, grapes and bread in the shop.

   (a) One of her dogs is called Millie. Another is called Bentley. Another one is called Buddy.
   Her dogs are called Millie, Bentley and Buddy.

   (b) She went to the library. She also went to the shop. She also went to the cinema.
   She went to the library, shop and cinema.

   (c) Barry's shirt was red. It was also white. It also had green on it.
   Barry's shirt was red, white and green.

   (d) Ciara likes swimming. She also likes badminton. She also likes volleyball.
   Ciara likes swimming, badminton and volleyball.

ACTIVITIES

F **Extension Ideas**

Use the library or internet to help you with the following exercise.

Write six interesting facts about the Amazon Jungle.

(a) _____

(b) _____

(c) _____

(d) _____

(e) _____

(f) _____

G **Writing Genre: Narrative Writing**

Fred and the other children have landed in the middle of the jungle. Imagine you are on an aeroplane that crashes into the unknown. Write your story below.

Title: _____

Where does the story take place? _____

When did the story happen? _____

What is the weather or climate like? _____

What can you see? _____

What can you smell? _____

What can you hear? _____

What can you touch? _____

What can you taste? _____

What is the landscape like? _____

How does this place make you feel? _____

_____

Now, use the template to help you write your story on page 130.

9 Missing from the Skies

A A Little Light Thinking

1. Write the first names of the Wright Brothers.
   (a) Orville   (b) Wilbur

2. What record did Amelia Earhart achieve in 1932?
   She became the first woman to fly across *the atlantic Ocean*

3. Where did Amelia and her family go on a day out when she was seven?
   Amelia and her family went to an amusement park

4. Where was John F. Kennedy Senior assassinated? Dallas in Texas

5. Who assassinated John F. Kennedy Senior? Lee harvey Oswald

6. Name the two passengers on board the aeroplane with John F. Kennedy Junior.
   (a) His wife   (b) his ex~~wife~~ sister

7. From where did Malaysia Airlines Flight 370 depart? Kuala Lumpur

8. How many people in total were on board the Malaysian flight? 239

B Deeper Thinking

1. Do you think the Wright Brothers were courageous men? Explain why.
   Well they did manage to build a flying machine that would sound like baloney to other people *in that time*

2. Why do you think it was such a huge deal for Amelia to get her pilot's licence?
   probally because when she was 7 she started loving aeroplanes.

3. Why do you think it was rare to have female pilots in 1920?
   Maybe because most females weren't intrested in that subject. *saw*

4. What do you think is meant by the line: *This was another tragedy to hit a family that was already all too familiar with heartache?*
   Probably since john F.kennedy S. was ~~assassinated~~ ~~as well~~ killed as well

5. Why do you think it is important for an aeroplane to keep in contact with air traffic control?
   It's because if they can pinpoint where they are so they don't collide.

6. Why do you think it is very difficult for investigators when searching ocean areas?
   Probably because Oceans are really big

Explain why you think that flying is one of the safest ways to travel.
Well there is pretty much no chance that it will hit another plane.

ACTIVITIES

C Vocabulary Work: Synonyms

Circle the word closest in meaning to the underlined word.

1. There have been some very underlined{unfortunate} air accidents.
   - (a) **unlucky** ✓
   - (b) favourable
   - (c) helpful
   - (d) involved

2. Thousands of flights reach their underlined{destination} every day.
   - (a) start
   - (b) source
   - (c) **terminal** ✓
   - (d) ~~end~~

3. Amelia Earhart was the first woman to fly underlined{solo} across the Atlantic.
   - (a) straight
   - (b) **unaccompanied** ✓
   - (c) fast
   - (d) aided

4. Her life came to a underlined{tragic} end.
   - (a) excellent
   - (b) fortunate
   - (c) cheerful
   - (d) **appalling** ✓

5. Visibility had underlined{deteriorated} badly during the flight.
   - (a) improved
   - (b) **worsened** ✓
   - (c) bettered
   - (d) brightened

D Comprehension Work: Cloze Procedure

Complete the story by filling in the blanks using words from the word box.

~~lightning~~	~~distances~~	~~direct~~	~~accident~~	~~world~~
~~horribly~~	~~around~~	~~flights~~	~~Wilbur~~	~~transatlantic~~
~~disappeared~~	~~aeroplane~~	~~records~~	~~solo~~	~~Beijing~~
~~wreckage~~	~~aviation~~	~~wedding~~	~~Atlantic~~	~~visibility~~

Air Travel

17/20

Orville and **Wilbur** ✓ Wright were the first people to build an **aeroplane** ✓ that could fly successfully. Up until that time, people had to travel long **distances** ✓ by ship. Today, people can travel to any part of the **world** ✓ in less than 24 hours by aeroplane. Soon, people will be able to travel from Ireland **direct** ✗ to Australia! Thousands of **flights** ✓ reach their destinations every day without a hint of trouble. It is said that you are far more likely to be struck by **lightning** ✓ than be killed in an air **accident** ✓. Sometimes, however, things can go **horribly** ✓ wrong.

Amelia Earhart broke many flying **records** ✓ and became the first woman to be on board a **transatlantic** ✓ flight. In 1932, Amelia also became the first woman to fly **solo** ✓ across the Atlantic Ocean. In 1937, her aeroplane **disappeared** ✓ in the centre of the Pacific Ocean while she was on a trip to fly **around** ✓ the world.

In 1999, John F. Kennedy Junior, his wife Carolyn and his sister-in-law Lauren travelled by aeroplane to attend a **wedding** ✓. During the flight, the weather and ~~solo~~ **aviation** deteriorated badly. Unfortunately, the **wreckage** ✓ of the aeroplane was discovered five days later, in the **Atlantic** ✓ Ocean.

One of the worst **visibility** ✗ disasters in history involved Malaysia Airlines Flight 370 flying from Kuala Lumpur, Malaysia to **Beijing** ✓ in China.

35

9 Missing from the Skies

E Word Sort: Thesaurus Work – Descriptive Words

Write the words from the word box under the correct headings below.

~~sorrow~~ ~~annoyance~~ ~~anxiety~~ ~~grief~~ ~~pleased~~
~~panic~~ ~~hatred~~ ~~fury~~ ~~delight~~ ~~melancholy~~
~~elation~~ ~~resentment~~ ~~begrudging~~ ~~joy~~ ~~unhappiness~~
~~covetousness~~ ~~dread~~ ~~temper~~ ~~jealously~~ ~~anguish~~
~~worry~~ ~~outrage~~ ~~cheerfulness~~ ~~concern~~ ~~rivalry~~

Sadness	Happiness	Anger	Fear	Envy
Sorrow	joy	fury	Panic	rivalry
unhappiness	Cheerfulness	hatred	worry	jealousy
dread	delight	outrage	concern	resentment
Melancholy	pleased	~~anxiety~~	~~anguish~~	~~temper~~
~~elation~~		annoyance	anxiety	Begrudging
~~anguish~~		grief		covetouness

F Grammar: Adjectives

An **adjective** is a describing word. It usually tells us more about a noun, e.g. The **huge** Boeing 777 landed at the airport. / Her family went to an **amusement** park in the city.

Write as many adjectives as you can for each of the following nouns:
e.g. **house**: huge, spooky, beautiful, old, haunted, spacious, deserted

1. clown: red nose, whiteface paint and silly clothes
2. dog: four legs, paws, horizontal body
3. street: shops, path
4. lady:
5. book:
6. criminal:
7. ocean:

G Extension Ideas

Use the library or internet to help you with the following exercise.
Abraham Lincoln and John F. Kennedy were presidents of the USA. There are a number of coincidences/similarities between them. Find six of them. The first one is done for you.

Abraham Lincoln	John F. Kennedy
Elected president in 1860	Elected president in 1960

H **Writing Genre: Persuasive Writing**

Many people have a fear of flying. Others can't understand why this is so.
You are asked to persuade your classmates why there is no need to be afraid of flying.
Complete the template below.

Title: **Why there is no need to be afraid of flying**

State your point of view: _____

_____

Reason 1: _____

_____

Reason 2: _____

_____

Reason 3: _____

_____

Conclusion: Give a summary of your main points. _____

_____

_____

Finally, I think that I have shown… _____

_____

_____

Now, use the template to help you write your argument on page 131.

10 Tilly and the Time Machine

A A Little Light Thinking

1. What did Mr Wormwood say he would push up the chimney after Tilly?
   He said he would push the broom

2. What fell off her clothes as she moved? Clouds of soot.

3. What did the twinkling church spire look like from the top of the building?
   The sun was on the church spire.

4. What parts of her body did she scrape on the way down?
   Her knees and elbow.

5. Where did Tilly land when she fell down the chimney? a grand fireplace

6. How many servants rushed into the room? 2

7. What job did Tilly say her dad did? she said he's an engineer

8. What future invention did the lady say that her dad had made?
   It was a time machine

B Deeper Thinking

1. Do you think it was a healthy job being a chimney sweep? Explain.
   No it wasn't because it probably was very hard and rose to breath without breathing the soot

2. Why was Tilly scared that Mr Wormwood would find out that she was a girl?
   Maybe because it was supposed to be a boy called Billy sweeping the chimney

3. Why do you think Mr Wormwood was using the broom?
   I think he was because he seemed very strict

4. How do you think the old lady felt when Tilly landed in her fireplace? Explain.
   Surprised shocked confused and probably couldn't breath

5. What sentence from the story tells us that the room in the palace was covered in soot?
   The room was filled with a black cloud

6. How do you think Tilly felt when she heard her dad had disappeared that morning?
   Sad full of despair but also probably a bit excited that she's closer to seeing him again.

CHALLENGE

What decade do you think Tilly has travelled back to? Explain.
I think the 1960s

C Vocabulary Work: Dictionary Meanings

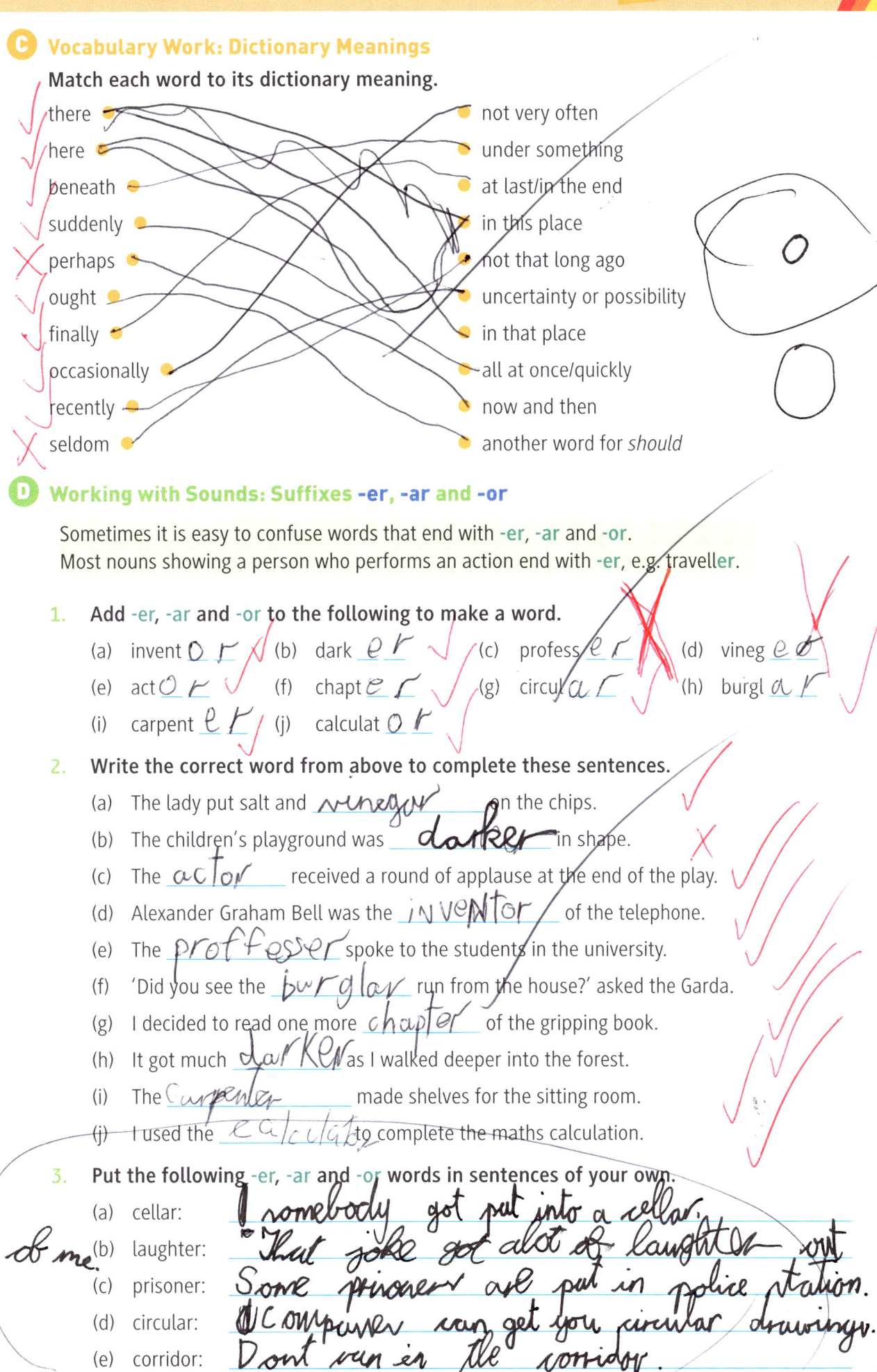

Match each word to its dictionary meaning.

- there — not very often
- here — under something
- beneath — at last/in the end
- suddenly — in this place
- perhaps — not that long ago
- ought — uncertainty or possibility
- finally — in that place
- occasionally — all at once/quickly
- recently — now and then
- seldom — another word for *should*

D Working with Sounds: Suffixes -er, -ar and -or

Sometimes it is easy to confuse words that end with -er, -ar and -or.
Most nouns showing a person who performs an action end with -er, e.g. travell**er**.

1. Add -er, -ar and -or to the following to make a word.
   - (a) invent **or**
   - (b) dark **er**
   - (c) profess **er**
   - (d) vineg **e**
   - (e) act **or**
   - (f) chapt **er**
   - (g) circul **ar**
   - (h) burgl **ar**
   - (i) carpent **er**
   - (j) calculat **or**

2. Write the correct word from above to complete these sentences.
   - (a) The lady put salt and _vinegar_ on the chips.
   - (b) The children's playground was _darker_ in shape.
   - (c) The _actor_ received a round of applause at the end of the play.
   - (d) Alexander Graham Bell was the _inventor_ of the telephone.
   - (e) The _proffesser_ spoke to the students in the university.
   - (f) 'Did you see the _burglar_ run from the house?' asked the Garda.
   - (g) I decided to read one more _chapter_ of the gripping book.
   - (h) It got much _darker_ as I walked deeper into the forest.
   - (i) The _carpenter_ made shelves for the sitting room.
   - (j) I used the _calculator_ to complete the maths calculation.

3. Put the following -er, -ar and -or words in sentences of your own.
   - (a) cellar: _somebody got put into a cellar._
   - (b) laughter: _That joke got alot of laughter out_
   - (c) prisoner: _Some prisoners are put in police station._
   - (d) circular: _A compasses can get you circular drawings._
   - (e) corridor: _Dont run in the corridor._

10 Tilly and the Time Machine

E Grammar: Verbs

A **verb** is an action or doing word, e.g. climb, look, talk, make, bring, calculate, etc.

Write each of the following sentences replacing the underlined verb with a more interesting verb in the word box.

~~quiver~~ ~~complete~~ ~~grip~~ ~~twinkle~~ ~~poke~~
~~alarm~~ ~~cascade~~ ~~clamber~~ ~~peer~~ ~~discover~~

1. The girl had to <u>climb</u> up through the chimney.
   The girl had to clamber up

2. I did not have enough time to <u>finish</u> my final examination.
   I did not have enough time to complete my final examination

3. 'Did you <u>find</u> the jewels that were hidden in the cave?' she asked.
   'Did you discover the jewels that were hidden in the cave?' she asked

4. She had a good <u>hold</u> of the railing as she climbed up the stairs.
   She had a good grip of the railing as she climbed up the stairs

5. He had to <u>stick</u> his head out the window to see the car coming.
   He had to poke his head out the window to see the car coming

6. She began to <u>shake</u> with fear after entering the old house.
   She began to quiver with fear after entering the old house

7. The water started to <u>gush</u> down the side of the mountain.
   The water started to cascade down the side of the mountain

8. 'I didn't mean to <u>scare</u> you when I shouted loudly,' he said.
   "I didn't mean to alarm you when I shouted loudly," he said

9. I saw the old lady trying to <u>look</u> out the window to wave me down.
   I saw the old lady trying to ~~alarm~~ peer out the window to wave me down

10. The diamonds seemed to <u>shine</u> brightly in the sun.
    The diamonds seemed to twinkle brightly in the sun

F Extension Ideas

Use the library or internet to help you with the following exercise.

Write five interesting facts about London.

(a) _____
(b) _____
(c) _____
(d) _____
(e) _____

G Writing Genre: Persuasive Writing

Tilly used the time machine to try and find her dad who was stuck in the past.

Write a persuasive essay for the following statement: *Tilly was right to go in the time machine to find her dad.* Discuss.

Title: **Tilly was right to go in the time machine to find her dad**

State your point of view: _____

_____

Reason 1: _____

_____

Reason 2: _____

_____

Reason 3: _____

_____

Conclusion: Give a summary of your main points. ____

_____

_____

Finally, I think that I have shown... _____

_____

_____

Now, use the template to help you write your persuasive essay on page 132.

11 Invasion

A A Little Light Thinking

1. What city were the Germans threatening to bomb? Rotterdam ✓
2. What did the children hear echoing down the street? The children heard stamping. ✓
3. To whose wedding was Anne going? Miep and Jan. ✓
4. Who spoke to the children at the end of assembly? ✗
5. What did Jewish children have to sew on their clothes? A golden star with the word Jood. ✓
6. What was the meaning of the word *Jood*? German for jew ✓
7. What did Anne pack in her bag? everything she saw ✗
8. Where was the secret annexe that they went to live in, situated? with Miep and Jan. ✗

B Deeper Thinking

1. Give two reasons why Anne lay awake most nights.
   (a) she was scared. ✗
   (b) she was worried about what ✗
2. Write one sentence from the story that shows the girls were trying to lead a normal life in spite of the war and bombs. At first, life carried on as normal. ✓
3. How do you think the teacher felt when she told the Jewish children they couldn't return to school? Explain. really annoyed and probably a bit sad.
4. Why do you think the Nazis made Jewish people sew the star onto their clothes? So everyone knew that you are ...
5. Why was being *called up* such a devastating thing to happen? Maybe because your about to lose your family.
6. Why do think the family did not take suitcases with them when they travelled to the annexe?

How do you think writing in the diary helped Anne while in the annexe?

ACTIVITIES

C Vocabulary Work: Alphabetical Order

Remember: When the first letters of words are the same, we must look at the second letter and so on in order to arrange them in **alphabetical order**.

Arrange the following word groups in alphabetical order.

1. ~~bicycle~~ ~~machine~~ ~~anchor~~ ~~coffee~~ ~~teapot~~
   anchor | bicycle | coffee | machine | teapot

2. ~~beginning~~ ~~balance~~ ~~biscuit~~ ~~butter~~ ~~blossom~~
   balance | beginning | biscuit | blossom | butter

3. ~~hunt~~ ~~harm~~ ~~hide~~ ~~head~~ ~~hole~~
   harm | head | hide | hole | hunt

4. ~~nature~~ ~~parade~~ ~~needle~~ ~~potato~~ ~~plate~~
   nature | parade | needle | plate | potato

5. ~~raced~~ ~~rushed~~ ~~rooms~~ ~~reading~~ ~~register~~
   raced | reading | register | rooms | rushed

6. ~~threaten~~ ~~thought~~ ~~together~~ ~~thinking~~ ~~talking~~
   talking | thought | threaten | thinking | together

D Working with Sounds: Homophones

Homophones are words that sound the same but have different meanings and spellings, e.g. some → sum / new → knew / hare → hair / night → knight / threw → through / clothes → close / dual → duel / you → yew.

Choose the correct homophone from the word box to complete each sentence.

| ~~know / no~~ | ~~threw / through~~ | ~~bare / bear~~ | ~~key / quay~~ | ~~Place / Plaice~~ |
| ~~rode / road~~ | ~~week / weak~~ | ~~profit / prophet~~ | ~~pane / pain~~ | ~~some / sum~~ |

1. I did not **know** which direction to go when I reached the crossroads.
2. The jockey **rode** the horse all around the field.
3. The burglar got into the house **through** the open window.
4. I felt **pain** after being in bed sick for a full week.
5. She walked on the soft carpet in her **bare** feet.
6. The company had to shut down because it wasn't making a **profit**.
7. The ship was docked in the **place** and the passengers disembarked.
8. The ball broke a **key** of glass in the window.
9. **week** is a type of fish loved by many people.
10. The children ate **some** of the cake during the picnic.

43

11 Invasion

E Grammar: Adverbs

An **adverb** tells us more about a verb. Most adverbs end in **-ly** or **-ily**, e.g. loud**ly**, laz**ily**, etc. We can make adverbs from adjectives, e.g. loud → loud**ly** / lazy → laz**ily**.

1. Change these adjectives into adverbs and write them in the correct sentences below.

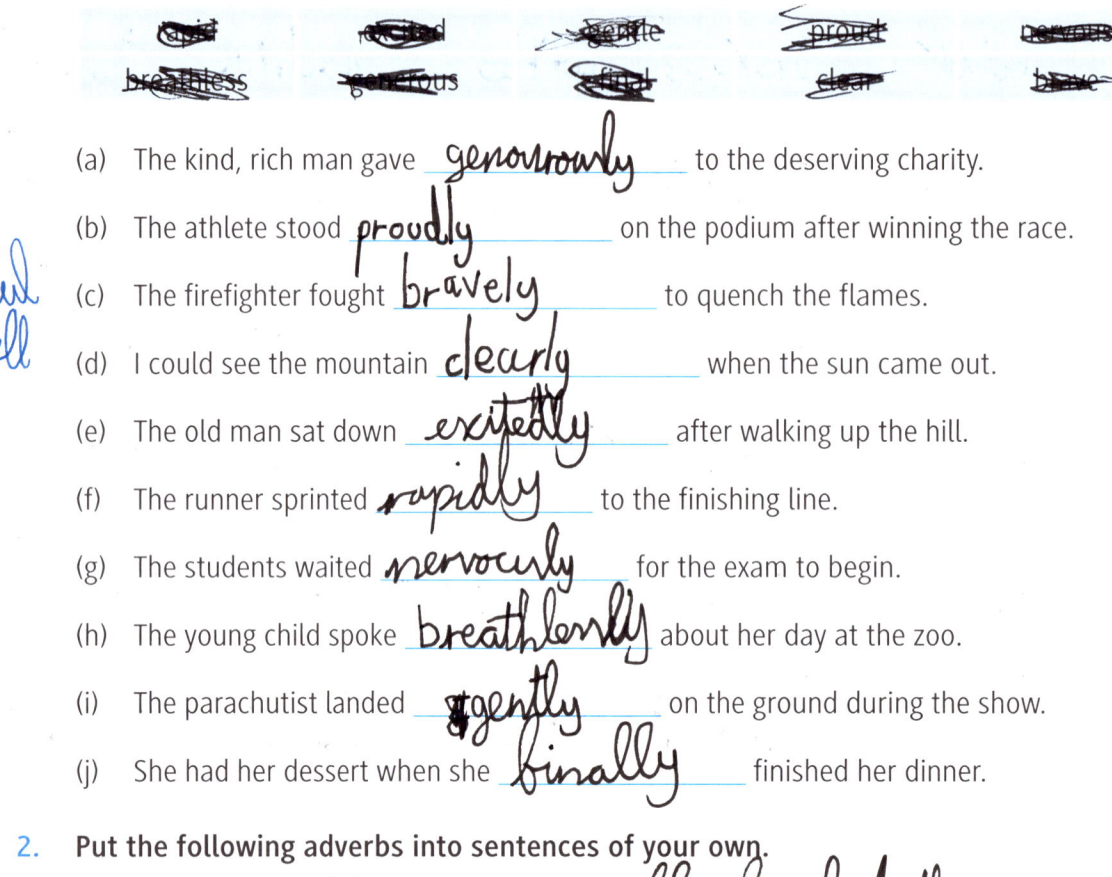

   ~~quiet~~   ~~excited~~   ~~gentle~~   ~~proud~~   ~~nervous~~
   ~~breathless~~   ~~generous~~   ~~rapid~~   ~~clear~~   ~~brave~~

   Saul Nicell

   (a) The kind, rich man gave _generously_ to the deserving charity.
   (b) The athlete stood _proudly_ on the podium after winning the race.
   (c) The firefighter fought _bravely_ to quench the flames.
   (d) I could see the mountain _clearly_ when the sun came out.
   (e) The old man sat down _excitedly_ after walking up the hill.
   (f) The runner sprinted _rapidly_ to the finishing line.
   (g) The students waited _nervously_ for the exam to begin.
   (h) The young child spoke _breathlessly_ about her day at the zoo.
   (i) The parachutist landed _gently_ on the ground during the show.
   (j) She had her dessert when she _finally_ finished her dinner.

2. Put the following adverbs into sentences of your own.

   (a) quickly: _The runner quickly finished the race_
   (b) angrily: _He angrily went out of the room_
   (c) silently: _He silently sneaked around_
   (d) happily: _He happily said that_
   (e) slowly: _The turtle slowly made his way._
   (f) loudly: _He said that extremely loudly._
   (g) easily: _He did it easily_
   (h) frequently: _He says that catchphrase frequently_
   (i) innocently: _He innocently stood there_
   (j) accidently: _He accidently broke the chair_

F **Extension Ideas**

Use the library or internet to help you with the following exercise.

Write six interesting facts about Anne Frank and her family.

(a) _____

(b) _____

(c) _____

(d) _____

(e) _____

(f) _____

G **Writing Genre: Writing to Socialise**

Imagine you are Anne Frank, hiding in the annexe with very little company. Write a letter to your friend, Sanne, telling her about your ordeal and what you hope will happen. Complete the template below.

Address: _____

_____

_____

Date: _____

Dear Sanne,

Greeting: _____

Paragraph 1: _____

_____

Paragraph 2: _____

_____

Paragraph 3: _____

_____

Farewell: _____

Sign off: _____

Now, use the template to help you write your letter on page 133.

45

12 Amsterdam

A A Little Light Thinking

1. What do the letters EU stand for? _European Union_
2. In what city in the Netherlands is the seat of government? _the Hague_
3. How many bridges are there in Amsterdam? _1281_
4. Why do some of the buildings in Amsterdam lean to one side?
   _____
5. Who became Chancellor of Germany in 1933? _Adolf Hitler_
6. Where was the annexe in which the Frank family lived?
   The Frank family lived in her dad's work building
7. How many bedrooms were in the annexe?
   two
8. How old was Vincent van Gogh when he painted his first piece?
   He was 27

B Deeper Thinking

1. Do you think windmills might be bad for the environment? Explain.
   I don't think they are that bad for the envirement.
2. Do you think it would be good to have a temperate climate? Why?
   Well its very mild so I think it would be a good idea
3. What are the benefits of using a bicycle as the main mode of transport?
   Well probably because you have a really view.
4. Why do you think Anne Frank's father decided to move to Amsterdam in 1934?
   Well
5. Do you think the secret annexe was a good hiding place? Explain.
   Well yeah there wasn't really any other option.
6. What sort of person was Vincent van Gogh? Give reasons for your answer.
   _____

CHALLENGE

Why do you think Vincent van Gogh's art only became popular after his death?

C Vocabulary Work: Synonyms

Remember: A synonym is a word or phrase that means the same or nearly the same as another word or phrase, e.g. reclaimed → recovered / dense → crowded.

Write the two words that are synonyms.

1. abandon, listen, leave, inhabit — (a) abandon (b) leave
2. enormous, young, minute, gigantic — (a) enormous (b) gigantic
3. rescue, calamity, disaster, destitute — (a) calamity (b) disaster
4. yearly, monthly, fortnightly, annually — (a) annually (b) yearly
5. enemy, friend, foe, soldier — (a) foe (b) enemy
6. reveal, conceal, show, artificial — (a) reveal (b) show
7. regretted, compelled, quarrelled, squabbled — (a) regretted (b) squabbled
8. famous, nobody, renowned, obstinate — (a) nobody (b) obstinate
9. quick, slow, rapid, pace — (a) quick (b) rapid
10. roam, stay, wander, direction — (a) roam (b) wander

D Comprehension Work: Cloze Procedure

Complete the story by filling in the blanks using the words from the word box.

Germany	mode	Belgium	Museum	Utrecht
half	polders	attractions	bicycle	population
reclaimed	Justice	capital	tourists	Criminal
dykes	Benelux	populated	government	headquarters

Amsterdam

The Netherlands was originally part of the __Benelux__ countries which consisted of __Belgium__, Luxembourg and the Netherlands. It borders Belgium, __Germany__ and the North Sea. A lot of its land has been __reclaimed__ from the sea as it is below sea level. These areas of land are called _____ and are protected from the sea by ridges or walls called _____.

The Netherlands has a _____ of approximately 17 million people. It is densely _____ as the country is only about __half__ the size of Ireland. The five biggest cities in the Netherlands are Rotterdam, Amsterdam, The Hague, _____ and Eindhoven.

Amsterdam is the _____ of the Netherlands but the seat of _____ is in The Hague. The Hague is also the _____ of the International Court of _____ and the International _____ Court.

The most popular _____ of transport in Amsterdam is the _____. There are more bicycles than people in the city. Amsterdam is famous for the Anne Frank House and the Van Gogh _____. Millions of people visit these _____ every year. It is a very popular city for _____ to visit.

47

12 Amsterdam

E Working with Words: Dictionary Meanings

Complete the following to show the dictionary meaning of the underlined words.

1. France borders _____
2. The climate _____
3. They reclaimed _____
4. The currency _____
5. The government _____
6. Their headquarters _____
7. The Chancellor _____
8. The annexe _____
9. They had an exhibition _____
10. The portrait _____

F Grammar: Apostrophes

When we want to show that something belongs to someone or something, we use an **apostrophe** followed by the letter **s**, e.g. Anne Frank**'s** diary. If the object belongs to more than one person, the apostrophe is put after the **s**, e.g. the girl**s'** bedroom.

Insert an apostrophe where it is needed in the following sentences.

1. The boys pencil lay on the floor.
2. All the ladies coats were in the hallway.
3. The childs clothes lay on the bed.
4. He looked very smart in his porters uniform.
5. My fathers wallet was discovered in the rubbish bin.
6. The cows tails swished from side to side.
7. The librarians chair was under the table.
8. The guards hat was on the chair.
9. The copybook lay on the teachers desk.
10. The girls dresses were in their wardrobes.

G Extension Ideas

Use the library or internet to help you with the following exercise.

Vincent van Gogh painted a very famous piece of art called *Starry Night*. Write three interesting facts or pieces of information about this painting.

(a) _____
(b) _____
(c) _____

ACTIVITIES

H Writing Genre: Writing to Socialise

Imagine you are on your holidays in Amsterdam. Write a postcard to your friend in Ireland telling them about your trip.

Name of friend: Ollie

Street and number: 0118 556 4432 ~~7753~~ bath avenue

Town:

County: Dublin

Postal code:

Country: Ireland

Date: 9/1/24

Greeting: Dear Ollie This is Saul

Paragraph 1: I have been here for 2 days so far so I'm gonna talk about it

Paragraph 2: On the first day ~~o~~ I came there I booked an airbnb and went to a restaurant.

Paragraph 3: On the second day I got ~~a~~ breakfast at a really yummy restaurant.

Farewell: Bye Ollie

Sign off: From Saul

Now, use the template to write your postcard on page 134.

13 Monkey Mayhem

A A Little Light Thinking

1. What was the professor's name? _____
2. Into what animal did Max change? _____
3. Who alerted the professor by squealing? _____
4. What was the troop of young baboons doing nearby?
   _____
5. To where did the baboons move in order to get shade from the sun?
   _____
6. Why did Max not eat the maggot?
   _____
7. What did the smudge on the horizon turn out to be?
   _____
8. What had his dad said about the buffalos?
   _____

B Deeper Thinking

1. What do you think the line: *The professor's legs acted as a flea magnet* means?
   _____
   _____
2. Why do you think Max had to fling his clothes off quickly before changing into an animal?
   _____
   _____
3. How did Max think that there was a storm approaching?
   _____
   _____
4. What sort of a person do you think Professor Slynk is? Why?
   _____
   _____
5. Why do you think the other baboons kept backing away from Max? Explain.
   _____
   _____

CHALLENGE

What problems did Max face after he changed into a monkey?
_____
_____
_____

C Vocabulary Work: Antonyms

An **antonym** is a word opposite in meaning to another word, e.g. soft → hard / stand → sit.

Rewrite the following sentences using an antonym for each of the underlined words.

1. He tried to <u>sit</u> as his bones felt soft and rubbery.
   _____

2. His face exploded from <u>inside</u> and fangs sliced through his gums.
   _____

3. Max chortled as a <u>distasteful</u> joy welled up inside him.
   _____

4. She stepped back and <u>slowly</u> recognised Max's bright, blue eyes.
   _____

D Working with Sounds: Suffixes -ic and -ick

Words of more than one syllable ending with a /k/ sound are spelt with **ic**, e.g. com**ic**, traff**ic**, etc. When adding **-ed** or **-ing** to one of these words, you must add a **k**, e.g. pan**ic** → pan**ick**ed. One syllable words ending with a /k/ sound are spelt with **-ick**, e.g. br**ick**, fl**ick**, st**ick**, etc.

Find the 10 -ic and -ick words in the wordsearch.

r	z	u	i	r	n	i	m	i	m	i	c	k	e	d
r	z	k	g	q	c	f	r	a	n	t	i	c	a	g
d	h	v	t	f	j	f	a	n	t	a	s	t	i	c
p	a	n	i	c	k	i	n	g	i	f	o	w	d	u
n	l	i	u	g	v	o	w	a	o	f	i	q	l	c
d	x	h	r	n	e	q	w	x	x	a	r	e	q	v
n	l	r	q	i	q	x	w	w	p	p	w	m	x	l
j	b	t	u	k	o	r	o	c	i	t	s	a	l	p
p	m	h	p	c	w	g	h	t	g	a	r	l	i	c
i	s	j	o	i	z	z	d	j	i	t	c	u	p	y
x	s	l	k	n	f	x	s	o	z	c	o	h	l	d
j	y	x	q	c	a	z	i	f	s	c	m	y	k	h
f	w	f	w	i	w	x	q	x	k	e	i	d	d	k
f	v	y	l	p	g	i	b	r	e	h	c	a	x	d
d	u	c	h	g	n	i	k	c	i	l	o	r	f	z

garlic →
comic ↓
fantastic ↓
frolicking ←
exotic ↘
picnicking ↑
plastic ←
mimicked →
panicking →
frantic →

13 Monkey Mayhem

E Grammar: Compound Words

Compound words are formed when two smaller words are joined to make a new, longer word with a new meaning, e.g. some + thing → **something** / card + board → **cardboard**.

1. Match the words to make compound words from the story. Write them.

   in • • where = _____

   any • • cup = _____

   back • • side = _____

   break • • cloth = _____

   every • • yard = _____

   hand • • place = _____

   saw • • one = _____

   farm • • wards = _____

   face • • fast = _____

   egg • • bag = _____

   fire • • dust = _____

2. Add a word to each of the following words to make a compound word.

   (a) after _____   (b) bed _____

   (c) day _____   (d) class _____

   (e) ear _____   (f) door _____

   (g) air _____   (h) foot _____

   (i) back _____   (j) gold _____

F Extension Ideas

Use the library or internet to help you with the following exercise.

Write five tasks a zoologist must do.

(a) _____

(b) _____

(c) _____

(d) _____

(e) _____

ACTIVITIES

G Writing Genre: Procedural Writing

In the story, Max has not eaten since breakfast time and his stomach is rumbling. Plan and write a recipe for one of the following breakfasts: (a) pancakes, (b) scrambled or boiled eggs, or (c) French toast. Complete the template below.

Title: _____

Aim: What do you want to do? _____
_____

Requirements: What materials are needed? _____
_____
_____

Method: Step-by-step instructions

Step 1: _____
_____

Step 2: _____
_____

Step 3: _____
_____

Step 4: _____
_____

Step 5: _____
_____

Step 6: _____
_____

Step 7: _____
_____

Did you achieve your goal? _____
_____

Now, use the template to help you write your step-by-step instructions on page 135.

14 Space Above Planet Mars

A A Little Light Thinking

1. What did the Martian moon *Phobos* resemble?

2. What was Olympus Mons?
3. What was a caldera?
4. How many obelisk pillars were there at the force field dome?
5. Who was piloting the crafts that passed close to Gilbert and Aoléon?
6. What were the buildings in the Martian megalopolis made from?

7. What word in the story means *moving sideways*?
8. Where did Aoléon dock her ship?

B Deeper Thinking

1. What is the meaning of the line: *It was like seeing it again for the first time through Gilbert's eyes*?

2. Why do you think that they had to contact Martian Control?

3. From what do you think they needed to guard the airspace around their colony?

4. Why do you think they built the city in the volcano, Olympus Mons?

5. What do you think Nebraska is like? Explain.

6. Why do you think the Martians could walk up the sides of buildings?

CHALLENGE

Why do you think Aoléon is bringing Gilbert to her planet?

C Vocabulary Work: Jumbled Letters

1. Use the clues to help you unscramble the letters to make words from the story. Write them.

    (a) plate placed under a cup — reucas — _____
    (b) vegetable killed by blight — otapot — potato
    (c) half of the earth — hispreehme — _____
    (d) move downwards — scddenede — descended
    (e) spews out lava and rock — alvonco — volcano
    (f) group of people living together — lonyco — colony
    (g) hard material used to make things — lamet — metal
    (h) the bigger part of a number — yamojrti — _____
    (i) the number of people in a place — nutioplapo — _____
    (j) A deep red colour — sircmon — _____

2. Unscramble the letters to make words from the story.

    (a) lapnte = p _____   (b) fribe = b _____
    (c) tmosrephea = a _____ (d) tmeamzaen = a _____
    (e) oewfrplu = p _____   (f) locasosl = c _____
    (g) frtca = c _____   (h) dremgee = e _____
    (i) ftcrleeed = r _____ (j) vereintd = r _____

D Working with Sounds: -ough Words

The letter string **-ough** can cause problems as it has a number of different sounds, e.g. rough (/uff/) / though (/oo/) / bought (/aw/) / through (/ew/) / dough (/ow/) / cough (/off/).

Put the following -ough words under the correct heading below.

though	through	bought	cough	rough	plough
ought	trough	bough	thought	fought	enough
dough	tough	doughnut	drought	although	

/oo/ sound	/off/ sound	/uff/ sound	/aw/ sound	/ow/ sound	/ew/ sound
(a)	(a)	(a)	(a)	(a)	(a)
(b)	(b)	(b)	(b)	(b)	
(c)		(c)	(c)	(c)	
(d)			(d)		

14 Space Above Planet Mars

E Grammar: Quotation Marks

Quotation marks are used to show someone's exact words. They go before and after a person's words. A comma, exclamation mark or question mark go before the final quotation mark, e.g. 'And this is where I live,' Aoléon said / 'Get out of my garden!' he roared / 'Why is the city inside a force field dome?' asked Gilbert.

Insert quotation marks, question marks, exclamation marks and commas in the following sentences.

1. I will finish up this meeting before five o'clock said the manager.

2. Where are you going on holiday asked the woman.

3. The train is at full capacity announced the conductor at the station.

4. May I borrow your pencil asked the boy during class.

5. When did you arrive in Ireland asked the tour guide.

6. Ouch exclaimed the young girl when she fell on the rough ground.

7. He is a fantastic dancer said Mary.

8. I am the best footballer in the school boasted Shane.

9. Can I help you with your work enquired the teacher thoughtfully.

10. Help she screamed at the top of her voice as she stumbled into the wall.

F Extension Ideas

Use the library or internet to help you with the following exercise.

1. Write three facts about any American states.

    (a) _____
    (b) _____
    (c) _____
    (d) _____

2. If you could live anywhere in America where would it be? Why would you live there? What would you do? What would you see?

    _____

G **Writing Genre: Procedural Writing**

Gilbert and Aoléon were navigating their way around Mars. Guide them step-by-step on the map, from Valles Marineris to Olympus Mons. You need to be very detailed with your directions so they don't go the wrong way. Use details from the story to help you.

Title: **Directions from Valles Marineris to Olympus Mons**

Aim: What do you want to do? _____
_____
_____

Method: Step-by-step directions

Step 1: _____
_____

Step 2: _____
_____

Step 3: _____
_____

Step 4: _____
_____

Step 5: _____
_____

Step 6: _____
_____

Step 7: _____
_____

Evaluation: Was it successful? _____

Now, use the template to help you write your step-by-step directions on page 136.

15 Space Exploration

A A Little Light Thinking

1. What are Russian astronauts called? Cosmonauts
2. What spacecraft did Yuri Gagarin use to orbit the Earth? Vostok 1
3. How long did it take Yuri Gagarin to orbit the Earth? 89 mins
4. What title did the Russian people give Valentina Tereshkova? Hero of the soviet union
5. What spacecraft did she use to orbit the Earth? Vostok 16
6. Who became President of the USA in 1960? John F. Keneddy
7. How long did Neil Armstrong spend on the moon? 2 1/2 hours
8. Who joined Neil Armstrong on the moon? Michael.C and Edwin Buzz.A
9. In what year is the first mission to Mars planned? 2025
10. What do the letters NASA stand for? National Aeronautics and space administration

B Deeper Thinking

1. Why do you think people are so curious about space?
   Well maybe because it can go on infinitly.

2. Why do you think it was so important for Yuri Gagarin to have good physical fitness for going to space?
   Well maybe because he would've been exhausted after the 0 gravity

3. Why do you think Valentina Tereshkova was called *Hero of the Soviet Union*?
   Well maybe because she was the first women to be in space and to orbit the earth

4. How do you think people around the world felt while watching the moon landing?
   They probally felt astounished and amazed about what they've achieved.

5. What do you think is the meaning of the line: *That's one small step for man, one giant leap for mankind*?
   Well maybe because every person in the world would take a normal step but the achievement was for mankind.

6. Why do you think the astronauts brought rocks and soil back to Earth with them?
   Probably for testing and maybe for souvenirs.

CHALLENGE

Why do you think it was mainly the Americans and Russians that led in space exploration?

ACTIVITIES

C Vocabulary Work: True or False?

Write true or false at the end of each of these statements.

1. An American space explorer is called a cosmonaut. *true*
2. Yuri Gagarin orbited Earth in 1961. *false true*
3. Valentina Tereshkova was born in Russia. *true*
4. Valentina Tereshkova was the second woman to travel into space. *false*
5. John F. Kennedy was president when the moon landing occurred. *true*
6. The *Eagle* landed in the Sea of Tranquility. *false*
7. The astronauts spent three hours on the moon. *true false*
8. Space exploration is a very safe job. *false*
9. NASA stands for National Aeronautics and Space Administration. *true*
10. NASA is planning to bring people to Mars in 2025. *false*

D Comprehension Work: Cloze Procedure

Complete the story by filling in the blanks using words from the word box.

~~Gagarin~~	~~impressed~~	~~travel~~	~~teacher~~	~~orbited~~
~~Sputnik~~	~~brilliant~~	~~board~~	~~Soviet~~	~~module~~
~~chosen~~	~~accepted~~	~~woman~~	~~climbed~~	~~cosmonaut~~
~~launched~~	~~admiration~~	~~Russian~~	~~astronauts~~	~~parachute~~

Space Travel

People who travel into space are usually called *astronauts*. In Russia, they use the term *cosmonaut* for space travellers. A small Russian satellite called *Sputnik* was launched in 1957 and so the Space Age began.

Yuri *Gagarin* was born in 1934. His maths and science *teacher* had flown an aeroplane during World War I and Gagarin was very *impressed* by this. He entered the army and began flight training. In 1960, he was selected for the *Russian* space programme. He was a *brilliant* student and was picked to be on *board* *Vostok 1* when it *orbited* the Earth in 1961. He became the first person to *travel* in space.

Valentina Tereshkova was a *Russian* cosmonaut. She had great *admiration* for Yuri Gagarin and also signed up for the Soviet space programme. Unusually, she could not fly but was *accepted* into the programme because she had completed 126 *parachute* jumps. In 1963, she was *accepted chosen* to pilot the spacecraft *Vostok 6* and became the first *women* to travel in space.

In 1969, the spacecraft, *Apollo 11*, was *launched* from The Kennedy Space Centre in Florida. Four days later, the lunar *module* part of the spacecraft, called *The Eagle,* landed on the moon. Neil Armstrong became the first man to actually walk on the moon when he *climbed* down the ladder to the surface of the moon.

15 Space Exploration

E Word Sort: Prefixes

Prefixes are placed at the start of a word to form a new word e.g. appear → **dis**appear.

Write the correct prefixes for each of the words below: **un-, dis-, ex-**

(a) _dis_ agree	(b) _dis_ appear	(c) _ex_ ample
(d) _ex_ port	(e) _ex_ clude	(f) _dis_ courage
(g) _un_ safe	(h) _dis_ cover	(i) _un_ civilised
(j) _un_ known	(k) _ex_ hale	(l) _ex_ pect
(m) _ex_ haust	(n) _un_ lucky	(o) _un_ dressed

F Grammar: Conjunctions

A **conjunction** joins words, phrases or sentences together, e.g. In 1957, the Soviet Union launched a small satellite into space called *Sputnik* **and** so, the Space Age began.

Choose the most suitable conjunction from the list for each sentence below.

    if   but   because   unless
    since   and   although   so

1. It rained all day, _____ the children remained inside.
2. 'She will go to the shop, _____ you ask her nicely,' said Mum.
3. He went to the doctor _____ he was feeling very sick.
4. The nervous boy will not go to the dentist _____ his mother brings him.
5. 'I haven't been to the cinema _____ last summer,' said the girl.
6. She still went walking, _____ it was pouring rain.
7. I went to the library to get a book, _____ it was closed.
8. The girl _____ boy both won prizes in the competition.

G Extension Ideas

Use the library or internet to help you with the following exercise.

Write five facts about the astronauts on board *Apollo 11*:
(a) Neil Armstrong, (b) Buzz Aldrin, and (c) Michael Collins.

(a) _____
(b) _____
(c) _____
(d) _____
(e) _____

ACTIVITIES

H Writing Genre: Free Writing

Write a story on the following picture. You are going to write for 10 minutes about the picture below. You can use words from the word box below to help you.
Don't forget to give your story a title.

space	gravity	rocket	lift-off	velocity
spacecraft	orbit	fuel	atmosphere	astronaut
launch pad	space station	earthbound	spacesuit	planets

Title: _____

Now, write your story on page 137.

16 The 1,000-Year-Old Boy

A A Little Light Thinking

1. What had hardly been invented in 1934?
   Refrigerator or the Telephon had hardly been invented

2. For how long had Alfie and his mother been living in Oak House?
   They have been living in the oak house for 80

3. Why did Alfie not give names to the chickens?
   Its because they sometimes eat the chickens.

4. Where was the grocery shop run by Mr and Mrs McGonagal?
   It was run in Eastbourne gardens

5. What had Jack's dad once done in Canada?
   His dad once shot a moose in Canada

6. What normally announced a customer's arrival in the shop?
   A doorbell

B Deeper Thinking

1. Why was it not a good thing if everybody knew about each other back then?
   Maybe Because if people were trying to keep secrets.

2. What do you think Biffa was? Explain why you think that.
   I think Biffa was Alfies dog.

3. Explain why you think Hexham was a good choice of town for Alfie to pick.
   Well because it is fourty miles away from there.

4. What excuse did Alfie give for not being in school that day?
   He said they had a week off for the mid-term break

5. What did Alfie say required him to spend longer periods of time with his *aunt*?
   Well because he wanted to spend more time with him or Jack

6. What damage do you think people with long memories could do to Alfie?
   They could Insault him

Why do you think Alfie was so hurt by Jack's words to Jean Palmer?
Well because he said bad things about Alfie. That might hurt his feelings

C Vocabulary Work: Dictionary Work

1. Match each word from the story to its dictionary meaning.

   televisions — a two-wheeled vehicle for cycling
   invented — something you do on a regular basis
   perfect — a table top in a shop
   bicycle — devices that show moving images or pictures
   routine — completely, totally; fully
   betrayed — created by ones own imagination
   entirely — a dairy product made from milk
   trousers — to have no flaws/correct in every detail
   cheese — to be deceived by a friend
   counter — a loose-fitting item of clothing for the lower body

2. Put each word from the word box in a sentence to show its meaning.

   moustache   suspicion   crouched   customer   eventually

   (a) The man grew a moustache
   (b) His suspicion grew bigger
   (c) He crouched down to be sneaky
   (d) I'm a usual customer at Kerala kitchen
   (e) He eventually got his rice.

D Working with Sounds: -sion Sound

Remember: Sometimes the letters **si** can sound like /zh/ in words ending in **-sion**, e.g. televi**si**on, explo**si**on, admi**ssi**on, colli**si**on, discu**ssi**on.

Put each word from the word box in the correct sentence below.

   occasion   decision   profession   mansion   possession   illusion
   permission   explosion   collision   passion   confusion   mission

1. 'What _____ would you like to have when you are older?' she asked.
2. The loud **explosion** terrified the people on the street.
3. The princess lived in a huge **mansion** in the country.
4. The players played with great **passion** in the final game.
5. It was just an **illusion** when the magician did the superb card trick.
6. I witnessed the **collision** between the car and the truck.
7. There was **confusion** in the theatre when the lights failed to work.
8. The thief was found in **possession** of the stolen goods.
9. The doctors went on a _____ to save the starving children.
10. Her wedding day was a special _____ for everybody.
11. 'We will make a **decision** about your behaviour later,' said Mum to Danny.
12. 'Have you got _____ to go to the cinema?' asked Gerry.

16 The 1,000-Year-Old Boy

E Grammar: Prepositions

Remember: **Prepositions** show the position of a noun in relation to something else, e.g. We grew stuff **on** a little patch of ground. / Biffa caught them all **within** a few weeks.

1. Choose the most suitable preposition from the word box to complete each sentence.

   ~~beside~~   ~~behind~~   over   from   ~~at~~   ~~inside~~
   near

   (a) There was a grocery shop ___in___ Eastbourne Gardens run by the McGonagals.
   (b) Jack helped in the shop ___behind___ the counter.
   (c) They threw stones ___at___ a tin can when they went down to the Links.
   (d) Every week there was a brass band playing ___on___ the bandstand.
   (e) Jack would even come ___to___ Alfie's house in the woods, sometimes.
   (f) He shrivelled ___inside___ because he had seen it all before.
   (g) He had moved ___to___ his position by the counter and crept out.
   (h) She put her slippers ___under___ the bed before going to sleep.
   (i) He walked too ___near___ to the river and he fell in!
   (j) It is often said that the cow jumped ___over___ the moon.

2. Put the following words plus prepositions in sentences of your own.

   (a) frightened of: _____
   (b) agreed to: _____
   (c) relied on: _____
   (d) aimed at: _____
   (e) tired of: _____

F Extension Ideas

Use the library or internet to help you with the following exercise.

1. Find out what the following items from long ago were and write about them:
   (a) wireless, (b) churn, (c) washboard, (d) vinyl player, and (e) wringer.

   (a) _____
   (b) _____
   (c) _____
   (d) _____
   (e) _____

2. What would be the advantages and disadvantages of living long ago?

G Writing Genre: Recount Writing

Imagine you are Alfie after hearing the conversation between Jack and Jean in the shop. Recount the story of *The 1,000 Year-Old-Boy* as a diary entry. Complete the template below.

Title: _____

Date: _____

Setting: _____

Who is the story about? _____

When did it happen? _____

Where did it happen? _____

What were they doing? _____

Why did it happen? _____

Event 1: _____

Event 2: _____

Event 3: _____

Event 4: _____

Afterwards, how did you feel? _____

_____

_____

Now, use the template to help you write your diary entry on page 138.

17 Parvana's Journey

A A Little Light Thinking

1. Where were all the other young men at this time?

2. What did Parvana say her name was?
3. What type of dwelling did Parvana and her father live in?
4. What did her father keep in his shoulder bag?
5. What did Parvana do as she walked away from her old home?

6. How many children were in the house when she arrived?
7. Where did the men sit when they came to the house where Parvana was staying?

8. Who had taken over the city of Kabul?

B Deeper Thinking

1. What lines show us the destruction caused by the Taliban?

2. Why do you think Parvana didn't trust anybody anymore?

3. Describe how the village looked as Parvana walked along with the men.

4. Why did the woman reach quickly for the burqa when the men came in?

5. Why do you think the men thought it wasn't safe for Parvana to search for her family?

6. Do you think Parvana kept travelling on? Explain.

CHALLENGE

Which of the following qualities help to describe the character of Parvana: (a) cowardly, (b) courageous, (c) intelligent, (d) dishonest, or (e) weak? What evidence from the story supports your choices?

ACTIVITIES

C Vocabulary Work: Synonyms and Antonyms

Remember: **Synonyms** are words of similar meaning, e.g. tall / lanky, while **antonyms** are words of opposite meaning, e.g. tall / short.

1. Write one word meaning the same as (synonym) and one meaning the opposite of (antonym) the words from the story, e.g. synonym → old / ancient; antonym → old / young.

Word	Synonym	Antonym
(a) stay	remain ✓	to go ✓
(b) hate	not like ✗	love ✓
(c) kind	nice	unkind ✓
(d) trust	uncareful	careful
(e) rough	hard	soft
(f) destroy	break	repair
(g) dark	darkness	light
(h) warmth	hot	cold
(i) ill	sick	fine permanent
(j) temporary		

2. Circle the word in each group that is not a synonym of the top word.

examine	enjoyable	attractive	genuine
scrutinise	pleasant	alluring	authentic
~~test~~	(displeasing)	beautiful	honest
(neglect)	entertaining	(repulsive)	(dubious)
audit	amusing	handsome	legitimate

D Working with Sounds: Suffixes -ery, -ory and -ary

Words ending in **-ery**, **-ory** and **-ary** can often have the same sound.

Add **-ery**, **-ory** and **-ary** to the following words and complete the sentences using that word, e.g. mem ____ → The boy lost his **memory** after the accident.

1. batt___ : I put a new _____
2. slipp___ : The road was very _____
3. secret___ : I saw the _____
4. fact___ : The workers made _____
5. jewell___ : The thief stole _____
6. libr___ : I borrowed _____
7. myst___ : The detective tried _____
8. hist___ : I find the study of _____
9. ordin___ : It was another _____
10. vict___ : The team _____

67

17 Parvana's Journey

E Grammar: Similes

Similes are used to compare two things. They usually include the words **like** or **as**, e.g. Weariness hit Parvana like a tank. / She ran like the wind. / She was as busy as a bee.

1. Choose a suitable word from the word box to complete the following similes.

| snow | owl | feather | rose | lead |
| bee | flash | bat | mule | swan |

(a) as light as a _____ (b) as white as _____
(c) as busy as a _____ (d) as stubborn as a _____
(e) as heavy as _____ (f) as red as a _____
(g) as graceful as a _____ (h) as blind as a _____
(i) as quick as a _____ (j) as wise as an _____

2. Put each simile listed above into a sentence of your own.

(a) _____
(b) _____
(c) _____
(d) _____
(e) _____
(f) _____
(g) _____
(h) _____
(i) _____
(j) _____

F Extension Ideas

Use the library or internet to help you with the following exercise.

1. List six items that you think would be important for Parvana to pack before travelling.
   (a) food   (b) her father's books
   (c) water   (d) clothes
   (e) pen and pencils (f) matches

2. If you had to live in a lean-to, what would you use to make it more comfortable?
   (a) tv
   (b) water dispenser
   (c) soft chair
   (d) food

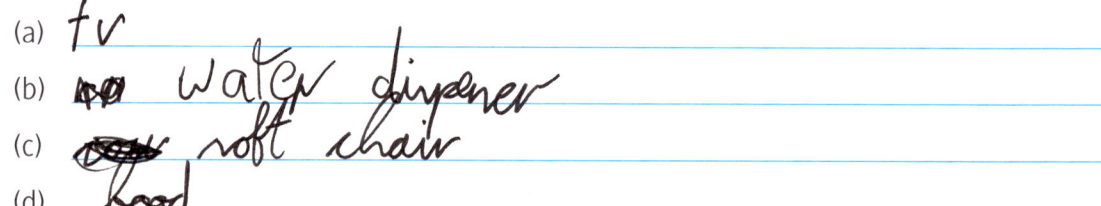

ACTIVITIES

G Writing Genre: Recount Writing

Imagine you are Parvana in Afghanistan. Recount the events of the day using the details from the story. Complete the template below.

Title: _____

Date: _____

Setting: _____

Who is the story about? _____

When did it happen? _____

Where did it happen? _____

What were they doing? _____

Why did it happen? _____

Event 1: _____
_____

Event 2: _____
_____

Event 3: _____
_____

Event 4: _____
_____

Afterwards, how did you feel? _____
_____
_____

Now, use the template to help you recount the events of the day on page 139.

18 I am Malala

A A Little Light Thinking

1. What is a landlocked country? _____
2. Name the capital city of Afghanistan. _____
3. Why was Malala targeted by the Taliban? _____
4. What was the name of Malala's school? _____
5. What language was Malala studying at school? _____
6. Who was Usman Ali? _____
7. Why had Malala started taking the bus to school? _____
8. Why did journalists come to talk to Malala and her father? _____

B Deeper Thinking

1. How were women treated differently from men in Afghanistan?
2. Do you think Malala was a courageous girl? Explain.
3. Why do you think the school has no sign on it?
4. What three reasons might the Taliban have for considering education a threat?
   (a) _____
   (b) _____
   (c) _____
5. What is a checkpoint? Why do you think they had them in Pakistan?
6. How do you think the men knew which girl on the bus was Malala?

CHALLENGE

Why do you think it is not safe for Malala to return to her country?

ACTIVITIES

C **Vocabulary Work: More Synonyms**

Write the word most similar in meaning to the underlined word(s) in each sentence.

1. Various groups tried to take over Afghanistan and gain control.
   (a) occupy ✓ (b) abandon (c) release (d) retreat

2. The women and girls were completely prohibited from travelling alone.
   (a) approved (b) authorised (c) forbidden ✓ (d) allowed

3. She almost paid the extreme price fighting for her right to an education.
   (a) ultimate ✓ (b) first (c) opening (d) auxiliary

4. We travelled in our usual motorcade of brightly painted rickshaws.
   (a) disorder (b) arrangement ✗ (c) dash (d) procession

5. My classes were spent reciting chemical equations.
   (a) learning (b) studying (c) chanting ✓ (d) solving

6. Malala was more troubled that they would target her father.
   (a) unperturbed (b) collected (c) concerned ✓ (d) composed

7. In truth, what happened was that the bus suddenly stopped.
   (a) belief (b) reality ✓ (c) fantasy (d) belief

D **Comprehension Work: Cloze Procedure**

Complete the story by filling in the blanks using words from the word box.

~~Afghan~~	~~imposed~~	~~home~~	~~control~~	~~fought~~	~~education~~	~~survived~~
~~refused~~	~~travelling~~	~~founded~~	~~driver~~	~~three~~	~~peaked~~	~~college~~
~~covered~~	~~information~~	~~Pakistan~~	~~Peace~~	~~received~~	~~youngest~~	~~educated~~

Malala's Story

Malala Yousafzai was born in 1997 in **Pakistan** ✓. The Taliban took **control** of her area. They **imposed** strict Islamic laws on the **Afghan** people. They did not allow women to be **educated** or to work outside the **home**. Women had to be **covered** from head-to-toe. Malala and her father **fought** for the right to a proper **education** for all children.

Her father **founded** a school to educate his daughter and other girls. As she was **travelling** to school one morning, by bus, two men approached the **driver** and asked him for **information** about some of the children.

The driver **refused** to give them any information. One of the men was wearing a **peaked** cap and looked like a **college** student. He proceeded to get on the bus to find Malala. He recognised her and shot her **three** times. Thankfully, she **survived** to tell her story. She **received** the Nobel **Peace** Prize in 2014 at 17 years old. She was the youngest person to receive the prize.

18 I am Malala

E Word Sort: Tired Words – Went

Complete the following using words from the word box to replace the tired words walked or went.

~~strolled~~   ~~limped~~   ~~shuffled~~   hobbled   crept
charged   staggered   ~~prowled~~   dashed   ~~marched~~

1. The firefighter (went) _dashed_ speedily to the fire.
2. The injured footballer (went) _limped_ slowly off the pitch.
3. The soldier (walked) _marched_ bravely down the street.
4. The old man (walked) _staggered_ awkwardly down the road.
5. The group of teenagers (walked) _strolled_ cheerfully around the park.
6. The small girl (went) _crept_ silently down the stairs.
7. The lame girl (went) _shuffled_ cautiously into the doctor's surgery.
8. The dizzy boy (walked) _hobbled_ clumsily into the swing.
9. The raging bull (went) _charged_ violently around the field.
10. The cunning thief (walked) _prowled_ sneakily around the house.

F Grammar: Possessive Pronouns

A **possessive pronoun** is a pronoun that shows ownership. They are used **without an actual noun**, e.g. That is not **yours**, it is **mine**! The main possessive pronouns are:
mine, **yours**, **his**, **hers**, **ours**, **yours**, **theirs**.

Write the possessive pronoun(s) in each of these sentences.

1. 'Is that yours or is it mine?' she asked.   (a) _yours_   (b) _mine_
2. 'The coats are not ours but theirs,' said the teacher.   (a) _ours_   (b) _theirs_
3. 'The ball is hers not his,' said Simona.   (a) _hers_   (b) _his_
4. The sweet is his but she thinks the sweet is hers.   (a) _his_   (b) _hers_
5. 'Is the iPad ours or is it theirs?' asked Danny.   (a) _ours_   (b) _theirs_
6. 'The cup is mine, not yours,' said Tina.   (a) _mine_   (b) _yours_
7. 'Mine is broken. Can I borrow yours?' she asked.   (a) _mine_   (b) _yours_
8. 'Theirs are red but ours are blue,' said Tim.   (a) _theirs_   (b) _ours_
9. 'The cap is hers, not his,' said Mum.   (a) _hers_   (b) _his_
10. Mum got yours and Dad got ours at Christmas.   (a) _yours_   (b) _ours_

G Extension Ideas

Use the library or internet to help you with the following exercise.

1. List six other types of Noble Prize.

    (a) _____ (b) _____
    (c) _____ (d) _____
    (e) _____ (f) _____

2. Seamus Heaney won a Nobel Prize. Write three interesting facts about his prize.

    (a) _____
    (b) _____
    (c) _____

H Writing Genre: Report Writing

Write a newspaper report about the shooting of Malala. Give your newspaper report an interesting headline. Complete the template below.

Title: _____

What happened? _____

Where did it happen? _____

Why did it happen? _____

When did it happen? _____

To whom did it happen? _____

Description: Give details about the shooting. _____

_____

Summarising comment: _____

_____

Now, use the template to help you write your newspaper report on page 140.

19 The Witch Next Door

A A Little Light Thinking

1. What did Mrs Murphy bring to the neighbour's house?

2. How did Rory change the subject of the neighbour at the dinner table?

3. What was making the dog so annoyed the next morning?

4. What three hobbies would Rory have liked his dad to have?
   (a) _____ (b) _____ (c) _____

5. What was the name of Dad's rabbit? _____

6. Who bought Dad his first magic set? _____

7. Who kicked the ball over the fence? _____

8. What did Mrs Blackwell offer the children to eat and drink?

B Deeper Thinking

1. What sentence tells us that the children think Mrs Blackwell is eccentric?

2. What kind of person do you think Granny Rose is? Explain.

3. Why do you think the birds appeared in Mrs Blackwell's garden every morning?

4. Give two reasons why Mrs Blackwell let the garden get so overgrown.
   (a) _____ (b) _____

5. Do you think the children were right to go into the garden next door? Explain.

6. Describe what Mrs Blackwell was wearing when the children entered the garden.

CHALLENGE

Do you think the woman next door is really a witch? Explain.

C Vocabulary Work: Word Links

1. Make word links of five words or as many as you can manage.
   Starting with the words given below, use the last two letters of each word to start the next word. Each word should have four letters or more, e.g.
   wit**ch** → ch**ee**se → se**v**en → en**tran**ce → ce**llar**.

   (a) homemade → _____
   (b) garden → _____
   (c) strange → _____
   (d) potato → _____
   (e) lecture → _____
   (f) piece → _____
   (g) launch → _____
   (h) regular → _____
   (i) sunshine → _____
   (j) tackle → _____

2. Write a word that will complete these word links.

   (a) covered → educate → _____ → argued → editor
   (b) hedge → ghost → _____ → eradicate → temple
   (c) welcome → measure → _____ → edible → learn

D Working with Sounds: Suffix -ture

The suffix **-ture** at the end of a word sounds like /**cher**/, e.g. crea**ture**, pic**ture**, depar**ture**, etc.

Solve the clues to complete the crossword. All words end with **-ture**.

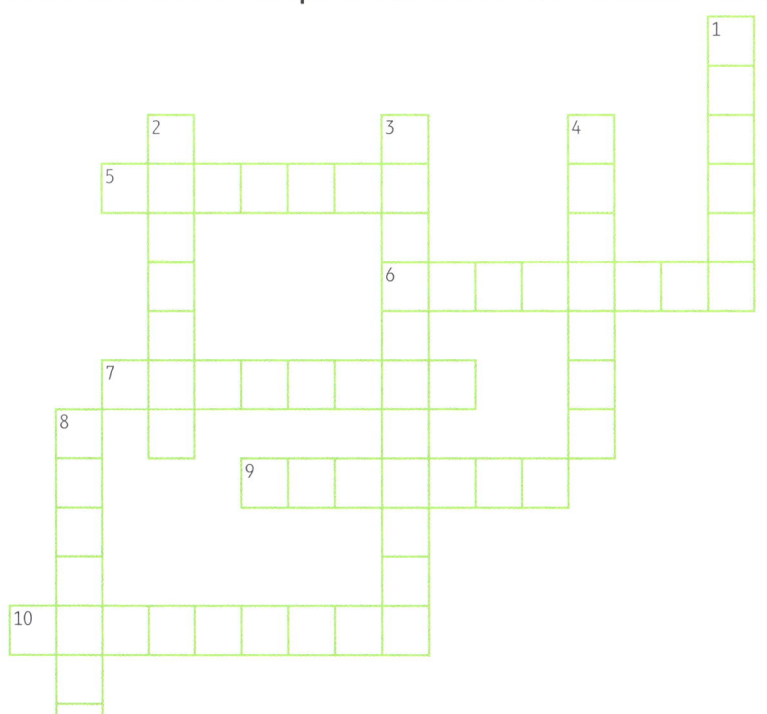

ACROSS
5. Can hang on the wall
6. A flat tyre
7. Any animal is one
9. A bird of prey
10. Chairs; table; presses

DOWN
1. Not past or present
2. Things mixed together
3. How hot or cold something is
4. To catch something
8. A talk or speech

75

19 The Witch Next Door

E Grammar: Metaphors

A *metaphor* is where comparisons are made **without** the use of **like** or **as**. Comparing the birds in the garden to **a group of soldiers taking orders from a commanding officer** is a metaphor. Birds can't be soldiers, but we understand the comparison!

1. Choose a suitable word from the word box to complete each metaphor below. Explain what you think each one means.

~~rollercoaster~~	~~money~~	~~ball~~	~~owl~~	~~bee~~
~~soul~~	~~blanket~~	~~star~~	~~pod~~	~~ears~~

   (a) The snow was a white __blanket__ on the ground.
   (b) The stormy ocean was a raging __star__ as it approached the land.
   (c) Her lovely voice was music to his __ears__ as she approached him.
   (d) Life is a __rollercoaster__ and we should take its ups and downs.
   (e) She is a shining __soul__ to all who come in contact with her.
   (f) It is said that time is __money__ and should not be wasted.
   (g) Laughter is the music of the __ball__ and is good for us.
   (h) He is a night __owl__ and sleeps all day.
   (i) She is a busy __bee__ and works tirelessly every day.
   (j) The friends are two peas in a __pod__ and will never be separated.

2. Write suitable words to complete these metaphors.

   (a) Jane was going to go on the rollercoaster but she got cold __feet__.
   (b) The stars are sparkling __diamonds__ in the sky.
   (c) He won some money so he pushed the boat __out__ and bought a new car.

F Extension Ideas

Use the library or internet to help you with the following exercise.

Write two pieces of information about two birds mentioned in the story.

   (a) _____
   (b) _____
   (c) _____
   (d) _____

G **Writing Genre: Report Writing**

Flocks of birds landed in Mrs Blackwell's garden every morning. Write a report on one of the following birds:

(a) magpie (b) crow (c) pigeon (d) starling

Title: _____

What does it look like? _____
_____

Where does it live? _____
_____

What does it eat? _____
_____

Interesting facts about it: _____
_____
_____

Summarising comment: _____
_____
_____

Now, use the template to help you write your report on page 141.

20 Alfie's World

A A Little Light Thinking

1. With whom did Alfie live? _____
2. Where did Alfie hide the letters that came from the dentist? _____
3. What job had his dad before becoming unwell? _____
4. What simple task became a struggle for Alfie's dad? _____
5. What did Alfie's dad call him? _____
6. In what type of house did they live? _____
7. In what type of world did Alfie and his dad live? _____
8. What did Alfie wish to play as he got older? _____

B Deeper Thinking

1. Why do you think Alfie was so scared of the dentist?
   _____
   _____

2. Do you think Alfie was an honest or dishonest boy? Explain.
   _____
   _____

3. Give two reasons why working in a coal mine might be bad for your health.
   _____
   _____

4. Alfie had a lot of responsibility for a young boy. Explain.
   _____
   _____

5. Why do you think Alfie's dad had to use imaginative stories to entertain his son?
   _____
   _____

6. Why do you think Alfie thought these daydreams were pointless by the end?
   _____
   _____

CHALLENGE

Which of the following qualities best describes the character of Alfie: (a) responsible, (b) selfish, (c) caring, (d) dishonest, or (e) weak? What evidence from the story supports your choices?
_____
_____

C Vocabulary Work: Occupations

An **occupation** is someone's job. The occupation of Alfie's dad was a **coal miner**.

Who am I? Solve the clues below to complete the crossword.
Use the words in the word box to help you.

~~photographer~~   ~~vet~~   ~~butcher~~   ~~doctor~~   secretary   ~~builder~~
~~waitress~~   ~~dentist~~   ~~postman~~   ~~nurse~~   ~~florist~~

1.	I take photos of all occasions.	ph	o tographer
2.	You come to see me when you're sick.	d o	c tor
3.	I run the office in a school or company.	se	c retary
4.	I sell meat.	B	u tcher
5.	I am a man who delivers your letters and packages every day.		p ostman
6.	I am a woman who serves food to your table in a restaurant.	W	a itress
7.	I look after sick animals.	ve	t
8.	I construct houses.	Bu	i lder
9.	I sell flowers.	fl	o rist
10.	I look after sick patients in hospital.		n urse
11.	I look after your teeth.	denti	s t

D Working with Sounds: Suffixes -ence and -ance

The letter **c** has an /s/ sound when it is followed by **e**, e.g. bal**ance** / exist**ence**.

Circle the correct spelling of the -ence and -ance words below.

(a) **entrance** / entrence
(b) **ambulance** / ambulence
(c) **sentence** / sentance
(d) **silence** / silance
(e) **fragrance** / fragrence
(f) **violence** / violance
(g) **difference** / differance
(h) **nuisance** / nuisence
(i) **performance** / performence
(j) **audience** / audiance

79

20 Alfie's World

E **Grammar: Contractions**

A **contraction** is a shortened version of a word using an apostrophe to replace the missing letter(s), e.g. could not → couldn't / I will → I'll / she will → she'll.

Rewrite the following sentences using the shortened form of the underlined words.

1. 'It <u>does not</u> really matter if you are late tomorrow,' said the teacher.

   'It doesn't really matter if you are late tomorrow,' said the teacher.

2. '<u>He will</u> be waiting at the main door when you arrive,' said Tina.

   'He'll be waiting at the main door when you arrive,' said Tina.

3. '<u>What is</u> wrong with the boy <u>who is</u> crying at the door?' asked Mum.

   'What's wrong with the boy who's crying at the door?' asked Mum.

4. 'I <u>cannot</u> believe that you said that out loud,' cried Amelia.

   'I can't believe that you said that out loud,' cried Amelia.

5. 'We <u>are not</u> going to meet you there at six o'clock,' retorted the bully.

   'We aren't going to meet you there at six o'clock,' retorted the bully.

6. '<u>You are</u> not supposed to be in that area,' ordered the park ranger.

   'You're not supposed to be in that area,' ordered the park ranger.

7. '<u>That is</u> the nicest dress that <u>I have</u> ever seen,' yelled the happy girl.

   'That's the nicest dress that I've ever seen,' yelled the happy girl.

8. '<u>They are</u> not finished their dinner yet!' roared the angry chef.

   'They're not finished their dinner yet,' roared the angry chef.

9. '<u>You have</u> not behaved that badly before,' sighed the boy's mother.

   'You've not behaved that badly before,' sighed the boy's mother.

10. '<u>I am</u> sure <u>she will</u> come with us to the concert,' chirped Arrianna.

    'I'm sure she'll come with us to the concert,' chirped Arrianna.

F **Extension Ideas**

Use the library or internet to help you with the following exercise.

Write three pieces of information about the legend of the Loch Ness Monster.

(a) _____

(b) _____

(c) _____

G Writing Genre: Persuasive Writing

Alfie hated going to the dentist. Write a persuasive argument for the following statement: *Alfie is right not to go to the dentist*. Complete the template below.

Title: **Alfie is right not to go to the dentist**

State your point of view: _____

Reason 1: _____

Reason 2: _____

Reason 3: _____

Conclusion: Give a summary of your main points. _____

Finally, I think that I have shown… _____

Now, use the template to help you write your persuasive argument on page 142.

21 Dramatic Rescues

A A Little Light Thinking

1. For what did people use the minerals they extracted from the mines?
   _____

2. Name two non-renewable resources that are mined.
   (a) _____ (b) _____

3. How many miners were trapped in the San José Mine? _____

4. How long did the miners spend underground? _____

5. From where were the young footballers and their coach rescued? _____
   _____

6. Where were they located nine days later? _____

7. What is thought to have caused the unfortunate rescue diver's death?
   _____

8. How many days were the boys trapped in the cave when the rescue mission began?
   _____

B Deeper Thinking

1. Why do you think these mined resources are so valuable?
   _____
   _____

2. Do you agree that mining is a hazardous job? Explain.
   _____
   _____

3. Why do you think it was important for the miners to have phone conversations with their families? _____

4. Do you think the rescuers did a good job rescuing the miners? Explain.
   _____
   _____

5. Many of the miners were traumatised afterwards. Explain why this could be.
   _____
   _____

6. Give two reasons why the Tham Luang cave rescue mission was so dangerous.
   (a) _____ (b) _____

CHALLENGE

What major challenges did the rescuers face on these two missions?
_____
_____
_____

C Vocabulary Work: Thesaurus Work

Circle the words that do not have the same meaning as the underlined words.

1. The earth is full of <u>resources</u> that can be mined.
   (a) assets   (b) riches   (c) reserves   (d) debt
2. The extraction of these <u>valuable</u> resources is a dangerous job.
   (a) costly   (b) expensive   (c) inexpensive   (d) treasured
3. There are many <u>hazards</u> associated with underground mining.
   (a) perils   (b) assurances   (c) risks   (d) threats
4. The mine <u>collapsed</u> and the miners were trapped.
   (a) strengthened   (b) crumpled   (c) caved in   (d) toppled
5. They <u>allowed</u> themselves two spoonfuls of tuna everyday.
   (a) denied   (b) sanctioned   (c) authorised   (d) permitted
6. The capsule was <u>manoeuvred</u> through a deep shaft in the ground.
   (a) disengaged   (b) navigated   (c) guided   (d) steered
7. The miners <u>gained</u> nothing financially from the disaster.
   (a) achieved   (b) benefitted   (c) forfeited   (d) obtained
8. The team was sheltering on a <u>ledge</u> above the water.
   (a) sill   (b) mantle   (c) hollow   (d) ridge

D Comprehension Work: Cloze Procedure

Complete the story by filling in the blanks using words from the word box.

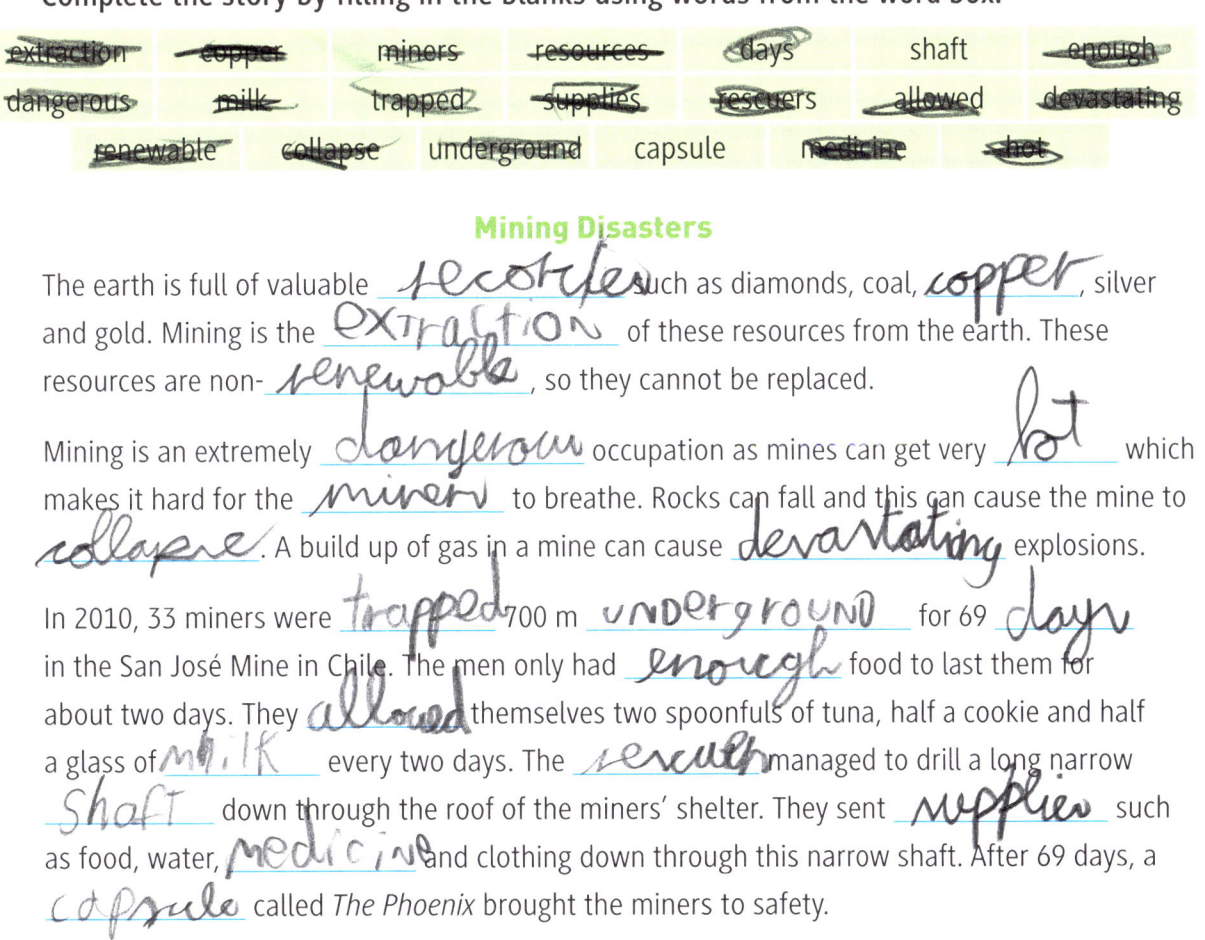

extraction · copper · miners · resources · days · shaft · enough
dangerous · milk · trapped · supplies · rescuers · allowed · devastating
renewable · collapse · underground · capsule · medicine · hot

Mining Disasters

The earth is full of valuable _resources_ such as diamonds, coal, _copper_, silver and gold. Mining is the _extraction_ of these resources from the earth. These resources are non-_renewable_, so they cannot be replaced.

Mining is an extremely _dangerous_ occupation as mines can get very _hot_ which makes it hard for the _miners_ to breathe. Rocks can fall and this can cause the mine to _collapse_. A build up of gas in a mine can cause _devastating_ explosions.

In 2010, 33 miners were _trapped_ 700 m _underground_ for 69 _days_ in the San José Mine in Chile. The men only had _enough_ food to last them for about two days. They _allowed_ themselves two spoonfuls of tuna, half a cookie and half a glass of _milk_ every two days. The _rescuers_ managed to drill a long narrow _shaft_ down through the roof of the miners' shelter. They sent _supplies_ such as food, water, _medicine_ and clothing down through this narrow shaft. After 69 days, a _capsule_ called The Phoenix brought the miners to safety.

21 Dramatic Rescues

E Word sort: Proverbs

Proverbs are old sayings that contain good advice with a lot of truth!

Match the following sayings to their meanings.

All that glitters is not gold • • People that you are friendly with for years are true friends

To have a heart of gold • • A person who is kinder and more pleasant than they seem to be from their appearance and manner

Make new friends but keep the old. Those are silver, these are gold •

Your health is your wealth • • The external look of something is not a reliable indication of what it's really like

A diamond in the rough • • Your health is the most important thing

• To be kind and considerate

F Grammar: Positive, Comparative and Superlative Degrees of Adjectives

Adjectives change their form when they are used to compare one thing with another, e.g. the shaft was narrow (**positive**), the pipe was narrower (**comparative**), the pencil is the narrowest (**superlative**) of all.

Complete the table below.

	Positive	Comparative	Superlative		Positive	Comparative	Superlative
1.	old	older		10.	happy		happiest
2.	wise		wisest	11.	lonely	lonlier	
3.	fast			12.	lovely		
4.	tall			13.	early		
5.	big			14.	lucky		
6.	bold			15.	good		
7.	sad			16.	bad		
8.	cold			17.	much		
9.	small			18.	little		

G Extension Ideas

Use the library or internet to help you with the following exercise.

Wind energy is an example of a renewable resource which is better for the environment. Find out six more renewable resources and describe what they are.

(a) _____

(b) _____

(c) _____

(d) _____

(e) _____

(f) _____

H Writing Genre: Persuasive Writing

Write a persuasive argument for the following statement: *Mining is a safe occupation.* Complete the template below.

Title: **Mining is a safe occupation**

State your point of view: _____

Reason 1: _____
_____

Reason 2: _____
_____

Reason 3: _____
_____

Conclusion: Give a summary of your main points. _____
_____

Finally, I think that I have shown… _____
_____

Now, use the template to help you write your persuasive argument on page 143.

22 The Television Game Show

A A Little Light Thinking

1. Why was Nate unable to pull the curtains in the lounge? _____
   _____

2. What three types of tinned food were in the kitchen?
   (a) _____ (b) _____ (c) _____

3. Who was the presenter of the game show? _____

4. From where in England were Stacey and Rob? _____

5. What prize did Nate's mum and dad receive as runners up?
   _____

6. What did Nate's mum do with the prize when his Dad moved out?
   _____

7. How much did Nate pay for the statue? _____

8. What was the answer to his crossword clue? _____

B Deeper Thinking

1. Describe what you think the cottage looked like. _____
   _____

2. How do you think having a television on would have kept Nate company?
   _____
   _____

3. Why do you think Nate liked the game show with his parents so much?
   _____
   _____

4. Explain why Nate would have bought the statue when he saw it in the shop.
   _____
   _____

5. Why do you think Nate was going to stuff Mrs Ellie-fant, the cuddly toy, in his bag when his mum arrived back? _____
   _____

6. What reasons could his mum have had for being away for so long? _____
   _____

CHALLENGE

Which of the following qualities best describes Nate's character:
(a) responsible, (b) brave, (c) caring, (d) confused, or (e) weak?
What evidence from the story supports your choices?
_____
_____
_____

C Vocabulary Work: Changing Letter Challenge

Complete the following words by changing one letter in the word each time, e.g. dog → cog → cot → cat.

1. bin	*pin*	*pen*	pet
2. van	*can*	*cat*	cot
3. sat	*pat*	*pan*	pin
4. lip	*tip*	*tap*	tan
5. bat	*bot*		box
6. rug	*wug*		wig
7. man	*mat*		sat
8. cat	*bat*	*bit*	big
9. dip	*jip*	*jop*	jog
10. dog	*hog*	*hig*	hit

Make up five Changing Letter Challenges of your own.

1.			
2.			
3.			
4.			
5.			

D Working with Sounds: Root Words

A root word is a word in its first and simplest form. A root word may be built up or have its meaning changed by adding a prefix or a suffix, e.g. phone means sound. In the word microphone, micro means small and phone means sound so, microphone → small sound.

Complete the table using the following root words twice.

Root Word	Meaning	Examples
1. photo	light	(a) photograph (b)
2. tele	far	(a) (b)
3. bio	life	(a) (b)
4. graph	to write or draw	(a) (b)
5. spec	to look	(a) (b)
6. aud	to hear	(a) (b)

22 The Television Game Show

E **Grammar: Masculine and Feminine Gender**

Nouns are said to be **masculine** gender if they refer to male creatures, e.g. **man**, **lion**, etc. Nouns are said to be **feminine** gender if they refer to female creatures, e.g. **woman**, **lioness**, etc. Some words, such as **actor**, may refer to all members of the acting profession, both male and female.

Use words from the word box to rewrite the following sentences with the masculine form of the underlined feminine words.

stallion	man	waiter	prince	His nephew
ram	king	he	He	barber
boy	his brother	gentleman	father	groom
his	actor	bull	his son	grandfather

1. She spoke to the princess in the castle courtyard.

2. The cow ran towards the mare in the large field.

3. The bride was nervous on her wedding day.

4. The woman gave her daughter some money to visit the zoo.

5. The actress played the role of a queen in the school play.

6. Her niece is a polite and friendly girl.

7. The ewe ran towards the lady in the field.

8. My grandmother loved swimming when she was young.

9. The waitress served her sister a magnificent meal.

10. My mother went to the hairdresser to get a hair cut.

F **Extension Ideas**

Use the library or internet to help you with the following exercise.

Find six pieces of information about an interesting game show of your choice.

(a) _____ (b) _____

(c) _____ (d) _____

(e) _____ (f) _____

ACTIVITIES

G **Writing Genre: Procedural Writing**

Nate loved watching the television game show *For Richer, For Poorer*. Think of a game you like to play. It can be (a) a card game, or (b) a board game.
Write the step-by-step instructions for a game of your choice.

Game 1

Title: _____

Aim: What do you want to do? _____
_____

Requirements: What materials are needed? _____
_____

Method: Step-by-step instructions

Step 1: _____
_____

Step 2: _____
_____

Step 3: _____
_____

Step 4: _____
_____

Step 5: _____
_____

Step 6: _____
_____

Step 7: _____
_____

Did you achieve your goal? _____

Finally, I think that I have shown... _____

Now, write step-by-step instructions for another game of your choice on page 144.

23 Kidnapped by a Yeti

A A Little Light Thinking

1. What is the young girl's full name? _____

2. What was her father wearing while asleep on the mountain? _____
   _____

3. Name the three boring things that girls were expected to do in England back then.

   (a) _____ (b) _____ (c) _____

4. What had wiped out all possible tracks of the yeti? _____

5. What did Lady Agatha think the yeti was when she gained consciousness?
   _____

6. In what way does the ear lid help the yeti? _____
   _____

7. How many toes did the yeti have? _____

B Deeper Thinking

1. Why do you think Lady Agatha and her father needed three porters?
   _____
   _____

2. Why do you think the Earl liked to bring his daughter travelling with him?
   _____
   _____

3. Why do you think the Earl thought his daughter had wandered off?
   _____
   _____

4. Give a reason why Lady Agatha thought she had died and gone to Heaven.
   _____
   _____

5. Describe the yeti's eyes as outlined in the story.
   _____
   _____

6. Why do you think the yeti father began to look anxious?
   _____
   _____

C Vocabulary Work: Prefixes and Antonyms

Add the prefixes dis-, un- or mis- to the words in the word box to make antonyms.

Remember: Antonyms are words of opposite meaning, e.g. safe → unsafe / known → unknown. Many opposites are got by adding the prefixes dis-, un-, mis-, e.g. obey → disobey / qualified → unqualified / place → misplaced.

1. Write antonyms for the following by adding the prefixes dis-, un- or mis-.

    (a) advantage: _____   (b) safe: _____
    (c) approve: _____   (d) trust: _____
    (e) behave: _____   (f) aware: _____
    (g) grace: _____   (h) obey: _____
    (i) taken: _____   (j) just: _____
    (k) necessary: _____   (l) chief: _____
    (m) connect: _____   (n) likely: _____
    (o) fortunate: _____   (p) lead: _____

2. Put the first 10 words listed above into sentences of your own.

    (a) _____
    (b) _____
    (c) _____
    (d) _____
    (e) _____
    (f) _____
    (g) _____
    (h) _____
    (i) _____
    (j) _____

D Working with Sounds: Rhyming Words Crossword

Rhyme occurs when word endings sound the same. The endings don't always have the same spelling, e.g. grew → blue / tough → stuff / noise → toys.

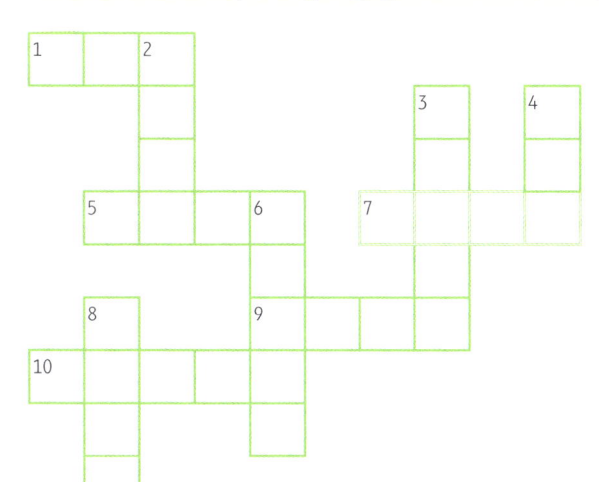

ACROSS
1. Dirt on the ground (flood)
5. Feeling scared (here)
7. Material from trees (could)
9. To not be on time (wait)
10. The liquid that can be squeezed out of vegetables and fruits (loose)

DOWN
2. To eat dinner (sign)
3. The opposite of to open (froze)
4. The colour of blood (said)
6. Used to draw a straight line (cooler)
8. To have good fortune (duck)

23 Kidnapped by a Yeti

E Grammar: Idioms

Idioms are common expressions used in conversation that have a different meaning from that which appears at first sight, e.g. on top of the world → to be extremely happy.

Write the correct meaning for each idiom underlined below.

(a) quarrelling
(b) to behave in a more responsible way
(c) to mind his manners
(d) feeling unwell

(e) accept the consequences
(f) caught in the act
(g) by a short margin
(h) someone cherished above all others

1. Liam is the <u>apple of his eye</u>.

2. The girl decided to <u>turn over a new leaf</u>.

3. The children just had to <u>face the music</u>.

4. Lisa was feeling <u>out of sorts</u> and stayed at home.

5. The two men were <u>at loggerheads</u> all the time.

6. She won the race by the <u>skin of her teeth</u>.

7. The boy was <u>caught red-handed</u>.

8. The lady told him to <u>mind his p's and q's</u>.

F Extension Ideas

Use the library or internet to help you with the following exercise.

Write the names of six major mountains in the world.

(a) _____ (b) _____

(c) _____ (d) _____

(e) _____ (f) _____

ACTIVITIES

G Writing Genre: Procedural Writing

Lady Agatha Farlingham was sleeping in a tent on the summit of Mount Nanvi Dar. Write step-by-step instructions on how to pitch a tent. Complete the template below.

Title: **How to pitch a tent**

Aim: What do you want to do? _____
_____
_____

Requirements: What materials are needed? _____
_____
_____

Method: Step-by-step instructions

Step 1: _____
_____

Step 2: _____
_____

Step 3: _____
_____

Step 4: _____
_____

Step 5: _____
_____

Step 6: _____
_____

Step 7: _____
_____

Did you achieve your goal? _____

Now, use the template to help you write your step-by-step instructions on page 145.

24 Unusual Creatures

A A Little Light Thinking

1. Where was the yeti crab discovered? _____
2. Describe what an elephant shrew looks like. _____
_____
3. What is a nocturnal animal? _____
_____
4. How did the glass frog get its name? _____
_____
5. Up to what height can an aye-aye grow? _____
6. What are primates? _____
_____
7. How many times does a bee hummingbird flap its wings per second? _____
8. Where can bee hummingbirds be found? _____

B Deeper Thinking

1. Why do you think the yeti crab wasn't discovered until 2005?
_____
_____

2. Explain how you think the elephant shrew got its name.
_____
_____

3. Do you think the paradise flying snake is a good name for the creature? Explain.
_____
_____

4. Why do you think the aye-aye is in danger of becoming extinct?
_____
_____

5. Give two reasons why the bee hummingbird might be mistaken for an insect.
   (a) _____
   (b) _____

CHALLENGE

Why do you think these creatures are unusual? Explain.
_____
_____
_____

ACTIVITIES

C Vocabulary Work: True or False?

Write true or false at the end of each of these statements.

1. A rabbit is an unusual creature. _____
2. The yeti crab was discovered in the Atlantic Ocean. _____
3. The elephant shrew is a small mammal. _____
4. The elephant shrew has excellent hearing, smell and eyesight. _____
5. The paradise flying snake moves into a 'c' shape. _____
6. The glass frog lives in Southern Mexico. _____
7. The aye-aye looks like a mixture of several creatures. _____
8. There is a large number of aye-ayes in Madagascar. _____
9. The robin is smaller than the bee hummingbird. _____
10. The bee hummingbird eats thousands of insects every day. _____

D Comprehension Work: Cloze Procedure

Complete the story by filling in the blanks using words from the word box.

creatures	lifetime	bacteria	fur	Earth
lobster	claws	visible	species	pointed
smallest	mistaken	Africa	rocky	twice
mammal	Caribbean	translucent	poisonous	rainforests

Unusual Creatures

Millions of creatures roam Planet _____. We are used to seeing many of these _____ every day such as cows, dogs, cats and horses. However, there are some creatures we might only see once in a _____, if at all.

The yeti crab is a small creature with a lot of _____ on its legs and _____. These claws contain _____ that it can use to remove _____ minerals from the water where it lives. Some say that it looks like a _____ with fur on it.

The elephant shrew is a small _____ found in _____. It gets its name from its long, _____ head and trunk-like nose, large eyes and ears. It lives in many habitats such as jungles, forests, woodlands and _____ mountains.

The glass frog gets its name from the layer of _____ skin on its stomach. Its heart, liver and intestines are clearly _____ to the human eye. It is an endangered _____ due to the cutting down of the _____ where they have their habitat.

The bee hummingbird is the _____ bird in the world. It is often _____ for an insect. It eats at least _____ its own body weight each day. It can be found in Cuba and neighbouring islands in the _____ Sea.

24 Unusual Creatures

E Word Sort: More Tired Words

The word said is overused and can make reading and writing very boring.

Choose a suitable word to make the following sentences more interesting.

exclaimed   stammered   explained   insisted   pleaded   shouted

1. 'I am late because the bus broke down,' _____ the boy.
2. 'Please let me go to the cinema,' _____ the teenager.
3. 'Ouch!' That was very sore,' _____ the patient.
4. 'You are definitely going the wrong way,' _____ the woman.
5. 'I… I am so nervous,' _____ John.
6. 'Get out of here NOW!" _____ the angry lady.

F Grammar: Indirect Speech

Direct speech is the exact words spoken by somebody and requires quotation marks, e.g. 'The aye-aye is a sign of death,' said the people from Madagascar.

Indirect speech is when the words spoken by someone are described by someone else, e.g. the people from Madagascar say that the aye-aye is a sign of death.

Change the following sentences to indirect speech.

1. 'I hate going to the doctor,' said Susan.

2. 'Who won that last race?' asked the referee.

3. 'It is time for dinner,' said Clara's mother.

4. 'Is it in your pencil case?' the teacher asked Ronan.

5. 'When are we going on holidays?' asked Sofia.

6. 'The actors in the play are excellent,' said the director.

7. 'Could I borrow your glue?' asked the child.

8. 'I am 11 years old,' said the boy.

9. 'Have you read that book?' asked the girl.

10. 'Who can recite the poem?' asked the teacher.

G Extension Ideas

Use the library or internet to help you with the following exercise.
Write the names of eight interesting creatures found in Ireland.

(a) _____   (b) _____

(c) _____   (d) _____

(e) _____   (f) _____

(g) _____   (h) _____

H Writing Genre: Explanation Writing

In this fact piece we looked at many unusual creatures. We have some unusual creatures in our own country. Write an explanation of how bees make honey.

Title: **How bees make honey**

Definition: What is honey? _____

How does it happen? _____
_____

Where does it happen? _____
_____

When does it happen? _____
_____

Why does it happen? _____
_____

What is it used for? _____
_____

Are there any interesting facts about bees? _____
_____

Special features: Is honey plentiful? _____

Now, use the template to help you write your explanation on page 146.

25 The Boy Detective

A A Little Light Thinking

1. What exciting job does Fletcher Moon have? _____
2. What was Bob Bernstein's first rule of investigation? _____
3. Name the school that the children went to. _____
4. How old was Doobie Doyle? _____
5. What was inside Fletcher Moon's small leather wallet? _____
6. What was the surname of the family that broke every rule? _____
7. Where was the agreed location for school fights? _____
8. What were the three most popular kinds of school fight?
   (a) _____ (b) _____ (c) _____

B Deeper Thinking

1. What lines from the story tell us that Herod was one of the *wild men* at school?
   _____
   _____

2. Why do you think it is important to stay *invisible* as a detective?
   _____
   _____

3. What sort of a character do you think Fletcher Moon is?
   _____
   _____

4. Describe what kind of person you think Doobie Doyle is.
   _____
   _____

5. Why do you think Doobie thought that the detective badge might not be real?
   _____
   _____

6. What sort of family was the Sharkey family? Explain.
   _____
   _____

CHALLENGE

Do you think Doobie Doyle was a trustworthy source to have? Explain.
_____
_____
_____

C **Vocabulary Work: Descriptive Sounds**

In the story *The Boy Detective*, the author describes the sights and sounds in the school yard. Certain words can be used to describe different sounds, e.g. the rustling of leaves.

1. Match the descriptive sounds to the nouns below.

| babble | clanking | crackling | creaking | rustling |
| howling | ticking | banging | patter | purring |

(a) The _____ of leaves   (b) The _____ of the wind
(c) The _____ of the stream   (d) The _____ of a clock
(e) The _____ of burning timber (f) The _____ of raindrops
(g) The _____ of a drum   (h) The _____ of chains
(i) The _____ of the engine   (j) The _____ of an old door

2. Put five of the above sound words into sentences of your own.

(a) _____
(b) _____
(c) _____
(d) _____
(e) _____

D **Working with Sounds: Suffixes -le, -el, -il and -al**

Sometimes words ending with -le, -el, -il and -al can have similar sounds. It can be difficult to decide on the correct spelling, e.g. normal, invisible, nostril, novel, etc.

Find the following words in the wordsearch.

h	i	d	e	p	m	l	e	l	v	a	l
o	l	p	t	o	a	e	v	a	t	n	l
r	a	u	q	s	n	a	l	t	o	i	e
m	n	z	w	s	u	u	a	i	w	m	v
e	i	z	f	i	a	a	n	p	e	a	o
l	m	l	w	b	l	f	i	s	l	l	h
g	i	e	l	l	o	w	f	o	e	y	s
g	r	e	c	e	x	b	c	h	n	o	q
u	c	s	c	r	i	b	b	l	e	y	x
r	n	l	r	t	r	a	v	e	l	z	b
t	f	u	y	h	l	e	w	e	j	f	i
s	x	f	g	v	o	w	e	l	v	e	m

hospital ↑   scribble →
criminal ↑   valuable ↙
animal ↓   vowel →
manual ↓   towel ↓
struggle ↑   shovel ↑
possible ↓   travel →
puzzle ↓   jewel ←

25 The Boy Detective

E Grammar: Abbreviations

We use an **abbreviation** to shorten words when a number of letters in that word are omitted, e.g. **Professor** Howard → **Prof.** Howard. If the last letter of an abbreviation is same as the last letter of the full word, we do not use a full stop at the end, e.g. **Sain**t Jerome's School → **St** Jerome's School.

1. Match the word to its abbreviation.

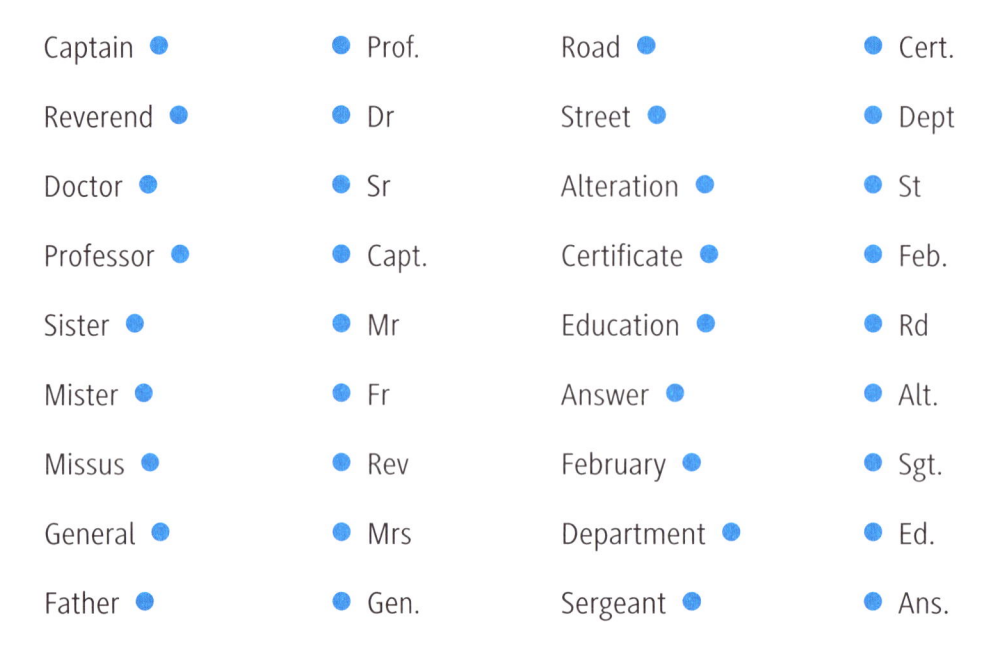

Captain •	• Prof.	Road •	• Cert.
Reverend •	• Dr	Street •	• Dept
Doctor •	• Sr	Alteration •	• St
Professor •	• Capt.	Certificate •	• Feb.
Sister •	• Mr	Education •	• Rd
Mister •	• Fr	Answer •	• Alt.
Missus •	• Rev	February •	• Sgt.
General •	• Mrs	Department •	• Ed.
Father •	• Gen.	Sergeant •	• Ans.

2. Write the full word/phrase for each of the abbreviations.

   (a) Mr: _____   (b) Ed.: _____

   (c) Rd: _____   (d) Fr: _____

   (e) Feb.: _____   (f) Gen.: _____

   (g) Sgt.: _____   (h) Prof.: _____

F Extension Ideas

Use the library or internet to help you with the following exercise.

List six things a detective would do during an investigation.

(a) _____

(b) _____

(c) _____

(d) _____

(e) _____

(f) _____

ACTIVITIES

G **Writing Genre: Explanation Writing**
Detectives have to use all their skills and knowledge of forensic science (the scientific method of gathering and examining evidence which is then used in a court of law) to help solve a crime. Write an explanation for how fingerprints can help solve a crime.

Title: **How can fingerprints help solve a crime?**

Definition: What are fingerprints? _____

How can they be used? _____
_____

Where can they be seen? _____
_____

When can it happen? _____
_____

Why does it happen? _____
_____

What are they used for? _____
_____

Are there any interesting facts about fingerprints? _____
_____

Special features: Are there times when studying fingerprints won't help detectives?
_____
_____

Now, use the template to help you write your explanation on page 147.

26 Mahmoud the Refugee

A A Little Light Thinking

1. Describe what Mahmoud looks like underneath the hoodie. _____
   _____
2. How old was Mahmoud's little brother? _____
3. When was the Old City of Aleppo built? _____
4. In what year did the Arab Spring come to Syria? _____
5. Who ruled Syria? _____
6. What did Mahmoud and his friend like to do in the evenings and at the weekends?
   _____
7. Why did Mahmoud and Khalid not go to the bathroom or playground at school?
   _____
8. What caused Khalid's death? _____

B Deeper Thinking

1. Why do you think Mahmoud tried to stay invisible in Syria?
   _____
   _____

2. Mahmoud describes his brother as being like a *robot*. What did he mean by that?
   _____
   _____

3. Why do you think Aleppo no longer looks like it did ten years ago?
   _____
   _____

4. In what way had things changed for Mahmoud in Syria?
   _____
   _____

5. What reasons do you think Mahmoud and Khalid had for drifting apart?
   _____
   _____

6. Why do you think Mahmoud didn't help the boy being beaten up?
   _____
   _____

CHALLENGE

Which of the following words help to describe the character of Mahmoud (a) responsible, (b) courageous, (c) cowardly, (d) caring, or (e) weak? What evidence supports your choices?
_____
_____

ACTIVITIES

C Vocabulary Work: American Words (Americanisms)

In America they call some of our everyday items by a different name e.g.
A mall is a shopping centre. / A movie theatre is a cinema. / The trunk of a car is the boot.

1. Match the American word with our name for the item.

   - counterclockwise
   - hood
   - trunk
   - cotton candy
   - parking lot
   - drugstore
   - french fries
   - trainers
   - checkers
   - garbage
   - sidewalk
   - vacation
   - popsicle
   - sweater
   - elevator

   - rubbish
   - lift
   - anticlockwise
   - carpark
   - holiday
   - jumper
   - boot (of a car)
   - footpath
   - chips
   - candyfloss
   - ice pop
   - bonnet (of a car)
   - draughts
   - chemist/pharmacist
   - runners

2. Write four more American words.

   (a) _____   (b) _____
   (c) _____   (d) _____

D Working with Sounds: Tricky Words Wordsearch

Some words can be tricky to spell, e.g. theatre, museum, route, government, answer, etc.

Find the following words in the wordsearch.

d	v	t	o	n	g	u	e	q	s	t	r	e	w	n
n	s	o	l	d	i	e	r	s	y	u	s	w	f	z
j	g	w	m	r	i	h	y	u	n	m	u	l	o	c
y	a	w	u	a	n	r	h	o	y	n	y	v	y	v
d	w	q	e	w	v	y	t	h	e	a	t	r	e	j
u	m	h	s	x	i	e	a	t	p	s	y	z	i	s
r	t	s	u	g	s	x	p	z	p	w	y	r	d	g
e	c	i	m	w	i	x	m	e	l	p	x	t	k	p
w	q	z	b	t	b	s	y	r	t	c	l	t	q	h
s	e	d	x	q	l	p	s	y	c	u	q	o	t	c
n	c	e	t	n	e	m	n	r	e	v	o	g	a	d
a	i	w	e	s	i	l	a	e	r	b	m	r	u	c
s	g	n	z	j	y	r	a	r	b	i	l	t	t	p
r	c	x	p	p	d	p	a	r	a	l	l	e	l	m
p	t	i	x	q	f	v	e	n	b	z	k	x	m	k

theatre →
museum ↑
invisible ↓
answer ↑
government ←
sympathy ↑
soldiers →
route ↖
strewn →
realise ←
library ←
tongue →
column ←
parallel →

26 Mahmoud the Refugee

E Grammar: Possessive Adjectives

A possessive adjective tells us more about a noun or pronoun showing us exactly who or what owns something. A possessive adjective acts like an ordinary adjective and must have a noun or pronoun with it, e.g. Mahmoud sat in the middle row of desks in his classroom. Possessive adjectives are as follows: my, your, his, her, its, our, their.

1. Put a suitable possessive adjective in each sentence below.

    (a) '_____ shirt is green but _____ shirt is red,' said Amelia.

    (b) '_____ dog is small but _____ dog is large,' said Danny.

    (c) _____ car is slow and they get really annoyed.

    (d) The dog is hungry and _____ bowl is empty.

    (e) _____ homework is on the table and we are happy.

    (f) 'Do you know where _____ pen is' asked the teacher?

    (g) She sat in the armchair in _____ sitting room.

    (h) He can't find _____ bag and doesn't know where he left it.

    (i) 'Are _____ shoes too small?' asked her mother.

    (j) 'I am getting a bicycle for _____ birthday,' said Cian.

2. Circle the possessive adjectives below.

    (a) My mother is here.
    (b) The boys lost their shoes.
    (c) This is his jersey on the chair.
    (d) We sold our car yesterday.
    (e) The bird hurt its wing.
    (f) Our cat is always licking its paws.
    (g) My shoes are new.
    (h) I don't have your phone number.
    (i) Her name is Melissa.
    (j) Don't forget to eat your lunch.

F Extension Ideas

Use the library or internet to help you with the following exercise.

1. Find out the capital cities of the following countries mentioned in the story.

    (a) Tunisia: _____   (b) Iran: _____

    (c) Libya: _____   (d) Yemen: _____

2. Write one interesting fact about each of the above countries.

    (a) _____

    (b) _____

    (c) _____

    (d) _____

ACTIVITIES

G Writing Genre: Writing to Socialise

Imagine you are Mahmoud living in Syria. Write an email to your friends who have left the country telling them about your life in Syria. Complete the template.

Email address: _____

Date: _____

Greeting: _____

Subject: _____

First, _____
_____

Next, _____
_____

After that, _____
_____

Finally, _____
_____

Farewell/sign off: _____

Now, use the template to write your email on page 148.

27 Syria

A A Little Light Thinking

1. What is the capital of Syria? _____
2. What did Abdulmajid see the next morning after the attack? _____
3. To what country did Abdulmajid and his family flee? _____
4. For what had Hudea mistaken Osman Sağırlı's camera? _____
5. What internet site did Bana and her family use to document the family's struggle?
   _____
6. What were Bana and her siblings doing just before their home was destroyed?
   _____

B Deeper Thinking

1. Why do you think desert regions are not suitable for growing crops?
   _____
   _____

2. What do you think the disadvantages of having a dictator as leader would be?
   _____
   _____

3. Do you think the government in Syria is helpful to their people? Explain.
   _____
   _____

4. Do you think Abdulmajid would have *a lot of work to do there* if he returned to Syria?
   _____
   _____

5. Why do you think Hudea mistook the camera for a weapon? Explain.
   _____
   _____

6. Do you think government leaders from around the world should help those in Syria? Explain.
   _____
   _____

CHALLENGE

Why would the people of Syria have lost trust in their government?
_____
_____
_____

C Vocabulary Work: More Synonyms

Find words from the story that have a similar meaning to the underlined words. The first letter of each word is given to help you.

1. The field is <u>neighboured</u> by the housing estate. b_____
2. Aleppo is the <u>biggest</u> city in Syria. l_____
3. High temperatures cause <u>dryness</u> in the region. d_____
4. He doesn't allow anyone to <u>question</u> his government. c_____
5. The people were maimed <u>for good</u>. p_____
6. One boy <u>remembers</u> his experience of the attack. r_____
7. The school they were attending was <u>ruined</u>. d_____
8. His father <u>constructed</u> a tent from wood and plastic. b_____

D Comprehension Work: Cloze Procedure

Complete the story by filling in the blanks using words from the word box.

Damascus	largest	president	Asia	crops	Muslims
Israel	supporters	dictator	ethnic	complicated	desert
problems	grazing	maimed	protestors	challenge	conditions

Syria

Syria is a country in western _____ bordered by Lebanon, Turkey, Iraq, Jordan, _____ and the Mediterranean Sea. Its capital city is _____, but Aleppo is the _____ city in the country.

Syria has many different _____ and religious groups. Sunni _____ make up the largest religious group. The land is poor and is mostly _____. Less than 10 percent of the land can be used for growing _____. This land is used for _____ animals.

The president is a _____ and nobody can _____ the decisions he makes. The Syrian people protested against their _____ in 2011. This took place because of their poor living _____. The president and his _____ attacked the _____ instead of trying to solve their _____.

In 2013, thousands were killed or _____ in the war. The situation in Syria is _____ and difficult to understand.

107

27 Syria

E Word Sort: Anagrams

Some words can change their letters around to make another word, e.g. rebuild → builder.

Write anagrams for the words with the same meaning as the phrases in the middle.

(a)	capes	above and around the Earth	
(b)	beats	a wild creature	
(c)	stare	drops of liquid from your eyes	
(d)	drawer	something you get for being good	
(e)	notes	a small rock	
(f)	stale	to rob	
(g)	panel	flies in the sky	
(h)	steer	plants that grow very tall	
(i)	weird	something broader	
(j)	pines	chord down your back	

F Grammar: Revision of Punctuation Marks

Rewrite the following sentences using proper punctuation.

1. Where do you live she asked

2. John likes to play basketball soccer and hurling

3. Ouch cried the young girl after she fell

4. Where do you think you are going demanded the man

5. That is Marys book on the ground said the little girl

6. Sarah went to the shop and bought eggs milk cheese and butter

7. What is your favourite book asked Ann

8. Stop shouted the guard as the thief ran down the road

9. Don't put the girls jacket in the wardrobe

10. I like Irish English maths and history at school

ACTIVITIES

G Extension Ideas

Use the library or internet to help you with the following exercise.

Write the names of six countries to which refugees might flee.

(a) _____   (b) _____

(c) _____   (d) _____

(e) _____   (f) _____

H Writing Genre: Writing to Socialise

Imagine you are Bana. Plan and write a message you would leave on Twitter for people to read about your life and how you feel. Complete the template.

Title: _____

Date: _____

Greeting: _____

Subject: _____

First, _____

Next, _____

After that, _____

Finally, _____

Sign off: _____

Now, use the template to help you write your message on Twitter on page 149.

28 Harry Potter Goes to Hogwarts

A A Little Light Thinking

1. What did Ron whack as the car was plummeting towards the ground?
   _____
2. Into what did they crash? _____
3. What was the name of Harry's owl that was shrieking in terror? _____
4. What had happened to Ron's wand? _____
   _____
5. Name Ron's rat. _____
6. What two words tell how the boys were feeling at the end of the extract?
   (a) _____ (b) _____

B Deeper Thinking

1. What lines tell us that the car wasn't working properly?
   _____
   _____
2. Were they lucky that they only hit the tree? Explain your answer.
   _____
   _____
3. Why do you think the tree was so mad?
   _____
   _____
4. Do you think Ron's dad will be mad? Explain.
   _____
   _____
5. Hogwarts is a magical castle. What lines from the story show this?
   _____
   _____
6. What sentence tells us that the boys were not arriving in triumph?
   _____
   _____

CHALLENGE

Do you think Harry and Ron will get in trouble? Explain.
_____
_____
_____

C Vocabulary Work: Tired Words Good / Bad

Replace the words good and bad in the following with words from the word box.

| rotten | delicious | pleasant | unsatisfactory | nasty |
| profitable | unfortunate | excellent | miserable | honest |

1. We ate a (good) _____ meal in the restaurant.
2. I had a (bad) _____ day at the beach because it rained all day.
3. He got a (bad) _____ cut on his knee while climbing the tree.
4. It was a (good) _____ company as it was making lots of money.
5. She is an (good) _____ student in every way possible.
6. 'That work is (bad) _____ and will have to be redone,' said the teacher.
7. She had (bad) _____ luck when she broke her leg before the final.
9. The girl was (good) _____ because she returned the money she found.
9. I had a very (good) _____ day at the zoo with my family.
10. One of the apples in the box was (bad) _____ and was inedible.

D Working with Sounds: Homonyms

Homonyms are words that are spelled the same but have different meanings, e.g. bonnet: the front of a car / a hat tied under the chin.

1. Write the homonym described below.

(a)	The hard outer covering of a tree	
(b)	The noise a dog makes	_____
(a)	A season in the year	
(b)	To move or jump suddenly	_____
(a)	To gesture goodbye with your hand	
(b)	A body of water curling into an arched form	_____
(a)	To squeeze or pack tightly into a small space	
(b)	A sticky sweet food put on bread	_____
(a)	A game	
(b)	Used to light a fire	_____
(a)	Used to draw a straight line	
(b)	Someone in control of a country	_____
(a)	A green area where you go to play	
(b)	What you do with your car before getting out	_____
(a)	The only mammal that can fly	
(b)	Used to hit a ball in cricket	_____

2. Give both meanings for the following homonyms:

(a) saw: (i) _____ (ii) _____

(b) right: (i) _____ (ii) _____

(c) sink: (i) _____ (ii) _____

28 Harry Potter Goes to Hogwarts

E Grammar: Revision of Speech

Write the proper nouns, common nouns, verbs, adjectives, adverbs and pronouns from the following sentences under the correct heading in the table below.

1. Jessie and Clara bought milk in the corner shop.
2. Cian and Danny walked quickly down the narrow road.
3. I ate a juicy, red apple for lunch.
4. He ran slowly and and lost the race in Galway.
5. They left the blue jackets in the school in Waterford.
6. 'We saw the tigers in the zoo,' she said.
7. Molly is a nice, friendly girl who works diligently.

Proper Nouns	Common Nouns	Pronouns	Verbs	Adjectives	Adverbs

F Extension Ideas

Use the library or internet to help you with the following exercise.

1. Write the names of six other characters from the *Harry Potter* series.

    (a) _____   (b) _____

    (c) _____   (d) _____

    (e) _____   (f) _____

2. Write the names of the four houses of Hogwarts in the *Harry Potter* series.

    (a) _____   (b) _____

    (c) _____   (d) _____

G **Writing Genre: Narrative Writing**

Harry and Ron travelled in a flying car back to school. Imagine you could borrow a flying car for a day. (a) Where would you go? (b) What would you do? (c) What would you see? Plan and write your story. Complete the template below.

Title: _____

Who is in the story? _____

Where does the story take place? _____

When does the story take place? _____

How do the characters get involved? _____

_____

_____

What is the conflict/problem? _____

_____

_____

_____

Resolution: How was the problem solved? _____

_____

Now, use the template to help you write your story on page 150.

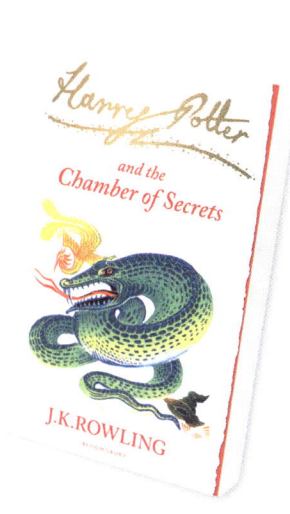

29 The Accident

A A Little Light Thinking

1. What did Bruno use to kick his feet against to make him go faster and higher?

2. What hit Bruno on the head?
3. Where had Bruno cut himself?
4. What was the waiter's name?
5. What colour was the liquid Pavel put on Bruno's cut?
6. What job had the waiter before he came to Bruno's house?
7. What does Bruno want to do when he is older?

B Deeper Thinking

1. Do you think the tyre was safe to use as a swing? Why?

2. Do you think Bruno was brave? Explain your answer.

3. What do you think the green liquid was?

4. Do you think Pavel was a good doctor? Give reasons for your answer.
   (a)
   (b)

5. What do you think is the meaning of the phrase: *Just because a man glances up at the sky at night does not make him an astronomer*?

6. Does Pavel seem like a happy person? Why do you think that?

CHALLENGE

Why do you think Pavel works as a waiter now and not as a doctor?

ACTIVITIES

C Vocabulary Work: Commonly Misspelled Words

1. Put these commonly misspelled words in alphabetical order.

   (a) restaurant
   (b) opportunity
   (c) mischievous
   (d) experience
   (e) embarrass
   (f) insurance
   (g) immediately
   (h) camouflage
   (i) february
   (j) relevant

   1. _____
   2. _____
   3. _____
   4. _____
   5. _____
   6. _____
   7. _____
   8. _____
   9. _____
   10. _____

2. Write words (a)–(e) above in sentences to show their meaning.

   (a) _____
   (b) _____
   (c) _____
   (d) _____
   (e) _____

3. Write the correct spelling of the following words from the story.

   (a) forhead or forehead: _____
   (b) heros or heroes: _____
   (c) begining or beginning: _____
   (d) address or adress: _____
   (e) visable or visible: _____
   (f) center or centre: _____

D Working with Sounds: Suffixes -ful, -some, -ment and -ness

Find the 10 words ending in -ful, -some, -ment or -ness in the wordsearch.

s	n	l	a	k	z	k	h	r	f	a	a	v	f	o
s	u	l	i	k	e	n	e	s	s	e	c	f	y	z
u	g	u	d	u	x	p	a	n	e	m	x	y	u	p
c	l	f	c	u	c	y	f	g	o	o	j	l	c	v
y	u	p	t	t	i	y	i	x	d	s	l	g	h	e
u	f	n	f	i	t	w	d	r	x	e	s	o	c	o
j	e	b	y	r	e	n	t	g	y	n	z	o	j	l
t	t	c	s	e	m	n	e	x	g	o	i	d	c	o
e	a	r	s	s	e	c	o	m	l	l	r	n	a	w
g	h	l	x	o	n	g	c	p	e	k	x	e	r	s
h	l	q	c	m	t	p	y	j	i	v	t	s	e	r
o	s	a	e	e	r	b	a	e	p	e	a	s	f	y
j	u	d	g	e	m	e	n	t	e	p	j	p	u	d
y	a	b	t	a	v	v	p	z	z	z	m	t	l	v
y	u	o	y	l	u	f	e	p	o	h	i	e	b	b

pavement ↖   excitement ↓
hateful ↑   lonesome ↑
tiresome ↓   goodness ↓
likeness →   careful ↓
hopeful ←   judgement →

29 The Accident

E Grammar: Revision of Conjunctions, Prepositions and Contractions

Write the conjunctions, prepositions and contractions from the following sentences under the correct heading in the table.

1. They'll be there early because they want to get a seat.
2. The boy walked to the shop while his friend stayed in bed.
3. I can't go but my sister will be there and she'll be very happy.
4. There's a ball near the wall.
5. The teacher went into the school and opened the windows.
6. I went towards the library when it was closed.
7. The ball was thrown through the window.
8. I've not seen him since the concert.
9. He'll put the book under the chair if it will stay hidden.
10. They said that they'd swim across the shallow river as it was swollen.

Conjunctions	Prepositions	Contractions

F Extension Ideas

You can use the library or the internet to help with the following exercise.

1. List six items that should go in a first aid kit.
    (a) _____ (b) _____
    (c) _____ (d) _____
    (e) _____ (f) _____

2. If someone fell and cut his/her knee, what steps should you follow?
    (a) _____
    (b) _____
    (c) _____
    (d) _____

3. If you were going to build a swing:
    (a) What materials would you use?
    _____
    (b) How would you put it together?
    _____

G **Writing Genre: Narrative Writing**

Bruno had a nasty accident when he fell from the swing and cut his knee. Imagine you had an accident. It might be falling from your bicycle, slipping down the stairs, etc. Write a story describing the lead up to the accident. Talk about what happened and how it was resolved. Complete the template below.

Title: _____

Who is in the story? _____

Where does the story take place? _____

When does the story take place? _____

How do the characters get involved? _____

_____

_____

What is the conflict/problem? _____

_____

_____

Resolution: How was the problem solved? _____

_____

_____

Now, use the template to help you write your story on page 151.

30 The Holocaust

A A Little Light Thinking

1. How many Jewish people were killed in Europe under Hitler's rule? _____
2. What name did Hitler call himself? _____
3. What was the first country that Hitler attacked? _____
4. What work had the prisoners to do in Auschwitz? _____
   _____
5. How many prisoners were crammed into the brick barracks? _____
6. On what did the prisoners in the camps sleep? _____
7. What did the filthy clothes of the prisoners look like? _____
   _____
8. How many Nazi leaders were put on trial in Nuremberg? _____

B Deeper Thinking

1. Why do you think Hitler had such a hatred of Jewish people?
   _____
   _____

2. Why do you think the German people voted for Hitler and the Nazi party in 1933?
   _____
   _____

3. Do you think *Kristallnacht* was a good name for the attack? Why?
   _____
   _____

4. How do you think the Nazis encouraged Jewish people to go to these camps?
   _____
   _____

5. Why do you think the Nazis kept the healthy people alive and killed the others?
   _____
   _____

6. Why do you think so few of the Nazi leaders were put on trial?
   _____
   _____

CHALLENGE

What sort of character was Hitler? Explain.
_____
_____

ACTIVITIES

C Vocabulary Work: True or False?

Write true or false at the end of each of these statements.

1. The Nazi party were a party in Austria. _____
2. World War I lasted from 1914 to 1918. _____
3. Hitler called himself the *Fuhrer*. _____
4. The Jewish people were Hitler's allies. _____
5. *Kristallnacht* means night of broken glass. _____
6. Britain and France declared war when Hitler invaded Poland. _____
7. Auschwitz was a camp built in Czechoslovakia. _____
8. The prisoners in the camps were fed very well. _____
9. The prisoners wore what looked like blue and white pyjamas. _____
10. There were over 100 leaders put on trial. _____

D Comprehension Work: Cloze Procedure

Complete the story by filling in the blanks using words from the word box.

Czechoslovakia	Austria	country	Vienna
Holocaust	compensation	businessman	Dachau
mines	persecute	starvation	farms
prisoners	worst	war	concentration

The Holocaust

The _____ is the name given to the killing of 6 million Jewish people during World War II. Adolf Hitler was born in 1889 in _____. He was from a wealthy family. His father wanted him to be a _____ but he only liked art and gymnastics, and failed to complete secondary school. He lived in _____, the capital of Austria. He painted postcards until he joined the German army during World War I.

The Germans lost the war and had to pay a huge amount of _____ to the countries they fought against. Anti-semites believed the Jewish people were to blame for losing the _____ because they didn't join the German army to fight for their _____. When Hitler invaded Austria in 1938 and _____ and Poland in 1939, Britain and France declared war on Germany. World War II had begun. Hitler made it one of his aims to _____ and torture the Jewish people. He built _____ camps where many Jewish people were executed. Many others died from _____ or disease. The first concentration camp was built in _____, in 1933. One of the _____ camps was Auschwitz, in Poland. Here the _____ went to work long, hard hours in coal _____ to mine coal for the Nazi factories. They also worked on _____ producing food for the Nazi army.

30 The Holocaust

E **Working with Sounds: Suffixes -ace, -ade, -ate, -age and -are**

Complete these word groups by adding one of the following suffixes: -ace, -ade, -ate, -age and -are. Each suffix should be used only once in each group.

1. casc____	volt____	comp____	grim____	demonstr____
2. priv____	comr____	sav____	aw____	surf____
3. bew____	marmal____	emigr____	pack____	embr____
4. furn____	sh____	eng____	inv____	pir____
5. decl____	clim____	pal____	saus____	lemon____
6. prep____	disgr____	chocol____	aver____	crus____
7. sol____	gren____	sl____	cott____	gl____
8. st____	gener____	tr____	aver____	par____

F **Grammar: More Punctuation**

Rewrite the following sentences using full stops, capital letters, question marks, exclamation marks, apostrophes, commas or quotation marks.

1. are those the girls coats asked mrs murphy

2. ouch cried the young girl when she caught her finger in the door

3. will you buy ham cheese and tomatoes in the shop asked mum

4. ill be back later from the cinema said the man

5. that is johns book over there on the table said the little girl

6. stop shouted the shopkeeper before the burglar ran out the door

7. do you prefer swimming hurling or reading asked the lady

8. youre not supposed to be there explained the Garda to the children

9. john boyne wrote the book *the boy in the striped pyjamas*

10. im sorry im late explained the breathless girl

ACTIVITIES

G Extension Ideas

Use the library or internet to help you with the following exercise.
Find out five more facts about Hitler and the Nazi party.

(a) _____
(b) _____
(c) _____
(d) _____
(e) _____

H Writing Genre: Free Writing

Look at the picture below. You are going to write for 20 minutes about this picture. You can write in any genre.

Title: _____

Now, write your story on page 152.

121

WRITING PAGES

Contents

Extract	Skill	Topic	Page
1. Something Nasty in the Lifts	Writing Genre	Recount Writing	123
2. The New School	Writing Genre	Recount Writing	124
3. Overcoming Disability to Succeed	Writing Genre	Report Writing	125
4. The Runaway Pram	Writing Genre	Report Writing	126
5. The Bear Cub	Writing Genre	Explanation Writing	127
6. The Stone Age	Writing Genre	Explanation Writing	128
7. The Changed World of Matt	Writing Genre	Narrative Writing	129
8. Lost in the Jungle	Writing Genre	Narrative Writing	130
9. Missing from the Skies	Writing Genre	Persuasive Writing	131
10. Tilly and the Time Machine	Writing Genre	Persuasive Writing	132
11. Invasion	Writing Genre	Writing to Socialise	133
12. Amsterdam	Writing Genre	Writing to Socialise	134
13. Monkey Mayhem	Writing Genre	Procedural Writing	135
14. Space Above Planet Mars	Writing Genre	Procedural Writing	136
15. Space Exploration	Writing Genre	Free Writing	137
16. The 1,000-Year Old Boy	Writing Genre	Recount Writing	138
17. Parvana's Journey	Writing Genre	Recount Writing	139
18. I am Malala	Writing Genre	Report Writing	140
19. The Witch Next Door	Writing Genre	Report Writing	141
20. Alfie's World	Writing Genre	Persuasive Writing	142
21. Dramatic Rescues	Writing Genre	Persuasive Writing	143
22. The Television Game Show	Writing Genre	Procedural Writing	144
23. Kidnapped by a Yeti	Writing Genre	Procedural Writing	145
24. Unusual Creatures	Writing Genre	Explanation Writing	146
25. The Boy Detective	Writing Genre	Explanation Writing	147
26. Mahmoud the Refugee	Writing Genre	Writing to Socialise	148
27. Syria	Writing Genre	Writing to Socialise	149
28. Harry Potter Goes to Hogwarts	Writing Genre	Narrative Writing	150
29. The Accident	Writing Genre	Narrative Writing	151
30. The Holocaust	Writing Genre	Free Writing	152

1 Something Nasty in the Lifts

WRITING PAGES

H Writing Genre: Recount Writing

Now, recount your story.

Title: _____

I Self Reflection

I was good at: _____

I need to do more work on: _____ Date: _____

2 The New School

WRITING PAGES

seemed
august   before.

G Writing Genre: Recount Writing

Now, recount your story.

Title: A suprise visit

I work at beecher prep middle school. first. one day a boy named August and he was a bit shy. Mr tushman told me all about August before. he was gonna check out the school and learn next. he came out of mr tushmans office so I gathered 3 kids but I think since he was a bit shy he might be overwhelmed and then when we were about to go in I heard him say "but Mum I don't wanna meet new people" He Said then I was really hesitant to go in.

Then, I eventually pushed myself to go in, when I did he was fine with it and he greeted everyone after that, the third kid julian suggested we go into the music room.

Finally, we went into the music room.

H Self Reflection

I was good at: _____

I need to do more work on: _____   Date: _____

3 Overcoming Disability to Succeed

WRITING PAGES

H Writing Genre: Report Writing

Now, write your report.

Title: **Michael J. Fox**

I Self Reflection

I was good at: _____

I need to do more work on: _____ Date: _____

4 The Runaway Pram

G Writing Genre: Report Writing

Now, write your report.

Title: **Report on a runaway pram**

H Self Reflection

I was good at: _____

I need to do more work on: _____ Date: _____

5 The Bear Cub

G Writing Genre: Explanation Writing

Now, write your explanation.

Title: **Why some animals have become extinct**

H Self Reflection

I was good at: _____

I need to do more work on: _____ Date: _____

6 The Stone Age

H **Writing Genre: Explanation Writing**

Now, write your explanation.

Title: **Why the Stone Age people needed fire**

I **Self Reflection**

I was good at: _____

I need to do more work on: _____ Date: _____

7 The Changed World of Matt

WRITING PAGES

G Writing Genre: Narrative Writing

Now, write your story.

Title: _____

H Self Reflection

I was good at: _____

I need to do more work on: _____ Date: _____

8 Lost in the Jungle

WRITING PAGES

G Writing Genre: Narrative Writing

Now, write your story.

Title: _____

_____
_____
_____
_____
_____
_____
_____
_____
_____
_____
_____
_____
_____
_____
_____
_____
_____
_____
_____
_____
_____
_____
_____
_____
_____

H Self Reflection

I was good at: _____

I need to do more work on: _____ Date: _____

9 Missing from the Skies

WRITING PAGES

H Writing Genre: Persuasive Writing

Now, write your argument.

Title: **There is no need to be afraid of flying**

I Self Reflection

I was good at: _____

I need to do more work on: _____   Date: _____

10 Tilly and the Time Machine

G Writing Genre: Persuasive Writing

Now, write your persuasive essay.

Title: **Tilly was right to go in the time machine to find her dad**

H Self Reflection

I was good at: _____

I need to do more work on: _____ Date: _____

11 Invasion

WRITING PAGES

G Writing Genre: Writing to Socialise

Now, write your letter.

Address: _____
_____
_____
_____

Date: _____

Dear Sanne,

Paragraph 1: _____
_____
_____
_____

Paragraph 2: _____
_____
_____
_____

Paragraph 3: _____
_____
_____
_____

Paragraph 4: _____
_____
_____
_____
_____
_____
_____
_____

H Self Reflection

I was good at: _____
I need to do more work on: _____ Date: _____

133

12 Amsterdam

WRITING PAGES

H Writing Genre: Writing to Socialise

Now, write your postcard.

Dear _____,

I Self Reflection

I was good at: _____
I need to do more work on: _____   Date: _____

13 Monkey Mayhem

G Writing Genre: Procedural Writing

Now, write your step-by-step instructions for your recipe.

Title: _____

Aim: What do you want to do? _____

Requirements: What materials are needed? _____

Method: Step-by-step instructions

Step 1: _____
_____

Step 2: _____
_____

Step 3: _____
_____

Step 4: _____
_____

Step 5: _____
_____

Step 6: _____
_____

Step 7: _____
_____

Step 8: _____
_____

Did you achieve your goal? _____
_____

Finally, I think that I have shown… _____
_____

H Self Reflection

I was good at: _____

I need to do more work on: _____ Date: _____

14 Space Above Planet Mars

WRITING PAGES

G Writing Genre: Procedural Writing

Now, write your step-by-step directions from Valles Marineris to Olympus Mons.

Title: **Directions from Valles Marineris to Olympus Mons**

Aim: What do you want to do? _____

Method: Step-by-step directions _____

Step 1: _____

Step 2: _____

Step 3: _____

Step 4: _____

Step 5: _____

Step 6: _____

Step 7: _____

Step 8: _____

Did you achieve your goal? _____

Finally, I think that I have shown… _____

H Self Reflection

I was good at: _____

I need to do more work on: _____ Date: _____

15 Space Exploration

WRITING PAGES

H Writing Genre: Free Writing

Now, write your story.

Title: _____

I Self Reflection

I was good at: _____

I need to do more work on: _____ Date: _____

16 The 1,000-Year-Old Boy

G Writing Genre: Recount Writing

Now, write your diary entry.

Date: _____

Dear Diary,

H Self Reflection

I was good at: _____
I need to do more work on: _____   Date: _____

17 Parvana's Journey

G Writing Genre: Recount Writing

Now, recount the events of the day.

Title: _____

H Self Reflection

I was good at: _____

I need to do more work on: _____ Date: _____

18 I am Malala

H Writing Genre: Report Writing

Now, write your newspaper report.

Title: _____

_____

I Self Reflection

I was good at: _____

I need to do more work on: _____ Date: _____

19 The Witch Next Door

G Writing Genre: Report Writing

Now, write your report.

Title: _____

_____
_____
_____
_____
_____
_____
_____
_____
_____
_____
_____
_____
_____
_____
_____
_____
_____
_____
_____
_____
_____
_____
_____
_____
_____
_____
_____

H Self Reflection

I was good at: _____

I need to do more work on: _____ Date: _____

20 Alfie's World

WRITING PAGES

G Writing Genre: Persuasive Writing

Now, write your persuasive argument.

Title: **Alfie is right not to go to the dentist**

H Self Reflection

I was good at: _____

I need to do more work on: _____ Date: _____

21 Dramatic Rescues

H Writing Genre: Persuasive Writing

Now, write your persuasive argument.

Title: **Mining is a safe occupation**

I Self Reflection

I was good at: _____

I need to do more work on: _____ Date: _____

22 The Television Game Show

WRITING PAGES

G Writing Genre: Procedural Writing

Now, write your step-by-step instructions for a game of your choice.

Title: _____

Aim: What do you want to do? _____

Requirements: What materials are needed? _____

Method: Step-by-step instructions _____

Step 1: _____
_____

Step 2: _____
_____

Step 3: _____
_____

Step 4: _____
_____

Step 5: _____
_____

Step 6: _____
_____

Step 7: _____
_____

Step 8: _____
_____

Did you achieve your goal? _____
_____

Finally, I think that I have shown… _____
_____

H Self Reflection

I was good at: _____

I need to do more work on: _____ Date: _____

23 Kidnapped by a Yeti

WRITING PAGES

G Writing Genre: Procedural Writing

Now, write your step-by-step instructions on how to pitch a tent.

Title: **How to pitch a tent**

Aim: What do you want to do? _____

Requirements: What materials are needed? _____

Method: Step-by-step instructions _____

Step 1: _____

Step 2: _____

Step 3: _____

Step 4: _____

Step 5: _____

Step 6: _____

Step 7: _____

Step 8: _____

Did you achieve your goal? _____

Finally, I think that I have shown… _____

H Self Reflection

I was good at: _____

I need to do more work on: _____ Date: _____

24 Unusual Creatures

WRITING PAGES

H   Writing Genre: Explanation Writing

Now, write your explanation.

Title: **How bees make honey**

I   Self Reflection

I was good at: _____

I need to do more work on: _____ Date: _____

25 The Boy Detective

G Writing Genre: Explanation Writing

Now, write your explanation.

Title: **How fingerprints can help solve a crime**

H Self Reflection

I was good at: _____

I need to do more work on: _____ Date: _____

26 Mahmoud the Refugee

G Writing Genre: Writing to Socialise

Now, write your email.

To: _____
Subject: _____
From: _____

Date: _____

Dear _____

_____
_____
_____
_____
_____
_____
_____
_____
_____
_____
_____
_____
_____

Kind regards,

_____

Send

H Self Reflection

I was good at: _____
I need to do more work on: _____ Date: _____

27 Syria

WRITING PAGES

H Writing Genre: Writing to Socialise

Now, write your Twitter message.

Twitter Post 1

Now, write another Twitter message.

Twitter Post 2

I Self Reflection

I was good at: _____

I need to do more work on: _____ Date: _____

149

28 Harry Potter Goes to Hogwarts

G **Writing Genre: Narrative Writing**

Now, write your story.

Title: _____

H **Self Reflection**

I was good at: _____

I need to do more work on: _____ Date: _____

29 The Accident

WRITING PAGES

G **Writing Genre: Narrative Writing**

Now, write your story.

Title: _____

_____
_____
_____
_____
_____
_____
_____
_____
_____
_____
_____
_____
_____
_____
_____
_____
_____
_____
_____
_____
_____
_____
_____
_____
_____
_____
_____
_____

H **Self Reflection**

I was good at: _____

I need to do more work on: _____ Date: _____

30 The Holocaust

WRITING PAGES

H Writing Genre: Free Writing

Now, write your story.

Title: _____

I Self Reflection

I was good at: _____

I need to do more work on: _____ Date: _____